THE FALKLAND ISLANDS
and their natural history

All illustrations by the author

DAVID & CHARLES
Newton Abbot   London

HIPPOCRENE BOOKS
New York

The west coast of Beauchene Island. Below the tussock-covered plateau a densely packed colony of black-browed albatross and rockhopper penguins

Ian J. Strange

THE FALKLAND ISLANDS

and their natural history

Foreword by HRH The Prince Andrew
The Duke of York

British Library Cataloguing in Publication Data

Strange, Ian J.
   The Falklands and their natural history.
   1. Natural history – Falkland Islands
   I. Title
   508.97'11   QH132.F3

   ISBN 0-7153-8833-9 (Great Britain)

Typeset by Typesetters (Birmingham) Ltd
Printed in Great Britain
by Butler & Tanner Limited, Frome and London
for David & Charles Publishers plc
Brunel House   Newton Abbot   Devon

Published in the United States of America
by Hippocrene Books Inc
171 Madison Avenue, New York, NY 10016
ISBN 0-87052-437-2 (United States of America)

*Port Louis and the
inner Careenage
harbour*

Contents

BUCKINGHAM PALACE

My first visit to the Falklands Islands took place in an atmosphere not conducive to the peaceful contemplation of the abundant wildlife. The chaos and mess which is the inevitable aftermath of armed conflict appeared to have reduced the islands to a state from which they could never recover. However I did have some opportunity to look around and see that, outside the limited area of military activity, the natural beauty of the Islands was greatly enhanced by the many varieties of bird life, some of them unique to the area, which had made their home there. It was in fact the landscape and wildlife which I saw in the Falklands that encouraged me to take up photography seriously. I think anyone who looks at the superb photographs in this book will understand how I felt.

Two years later, and in more settled times for the islanders, I came back and was once again struck by the great beauty of the Falklands and how little it had actually been affected by the greatly increased population and by such modern invasions as the new airport.

I am delighted that this Guide to the Falkland Islands and their Natural History has been written; it will serve greatly to widen the knowledge of these Islands and might even inspire a few people to go and see for themselves.

[signature]

1987

Opposite:
Bow of the SS Great Britain

Pages 6–7:
Shepherd's house at Loch Head Pond, East Falkland

Pages 10–11:
Stanley. The coloured iron roofs of the little capital presenting a splash of colour against the subtle coloration of the surrounding landscape

Introduction

In the evening we reached the Jason Islands, on the NE of the West Falkland Islands. On passing the Jason West Cay, the westernmost of the group, a most pungent odour, compounded of guano and decaying fish, was wafted off to the ship, unmistakeable evidence of an extensive roosting place of many penguins or cormorants. At the same time we encountered a most remarkable tide rip. A little more than an hour later we were drifted by a very strong current unpleasantly close to Jason East Cay, and soon after one of the steep cones of Steeple Jason, upwards of one thousand feet high, formed a striking object, looming through the haze.

Such was the account written by the master of one of the earlier expedition ships in the 1800s. And here I was some 130 years later, experiencing the same journey.

For well over three hours we had been bucking, dipping and heeling over to such an angle that the deck was rarely free of swirling water. All around the cutter were foaming waves which continually broke over the boat in the most unpredictable manner. Time and again we had attempted to steer the vessel in such a way that the bows headed into the broken water but in vain. Instead we were being moved by forces below us over which we had little control. We estimated from our almost stationary position just off one of the Jason Islands that the boat's engine was pushing us at no more than one knot. It was like being in a sea whipped up by a gale, but there was insufficient wind to justify putting up our sails. Weather-wise it was a beautiful day with the sun beating down from an almost cloudless sky. I had known by reputation something of the tide rips in this region but this was my first experience of them. The sea's surface had changed quickly from the comparatively calm waters just out of West Point Island to this turbulent mass.

More amazing, however, was the sudden change in the amount of bird and animal life seen since we had entered the area of these tide rips. Every wave top appeared to be surmounted by the fluttering forms of prions as they dipped and scooped into the broken water, picking up food. Between the troughs of the waves countless numbers of black-browed albatross soared just above the water, occasionally dropping onto the sea to grasp some seemingly invisible prey just below the surface. At one point we crossed an area where a group of fur seal were porpoising back and forth through the disturbed water, so intent on feeding that they took little or no notice of our boat.

Some hours later, when I had landed on one of the Jason Islands I, too, became aware of the 'most pungent odour' but, unlike those earlier voyagers, I was to stand overlooking an enormous seabird colony, almost certainly the same one described one hundred and thirty years before. I had landed on the lee of the island and, although the air was still, there was that unmistakeable stench. I pushed through the thick tussock grass covering the perimeter of the island which was over 1.8m (6ft) tall in many parts and made my way towards the opposite shoreline, guided by a roar which I thought came from the sea.

Breaking through the outer fringe of the tussock, I was hardly able to take in the sight that now lay before me: a mass of black-browed albatross and rockhopper penguins so densely packed that nesting birds could stretch out and touch each other. The roaring was not that of the sea but a discord of sound from this huge rookery. The colony of birds took up a large area of the foreshore, being perhaps 274m (300yd) or more in width and over 1.5km (1 mile) long.

Map of Falkland Archipelago showing Mount Pleasant Airport and Stanley, the capital

12

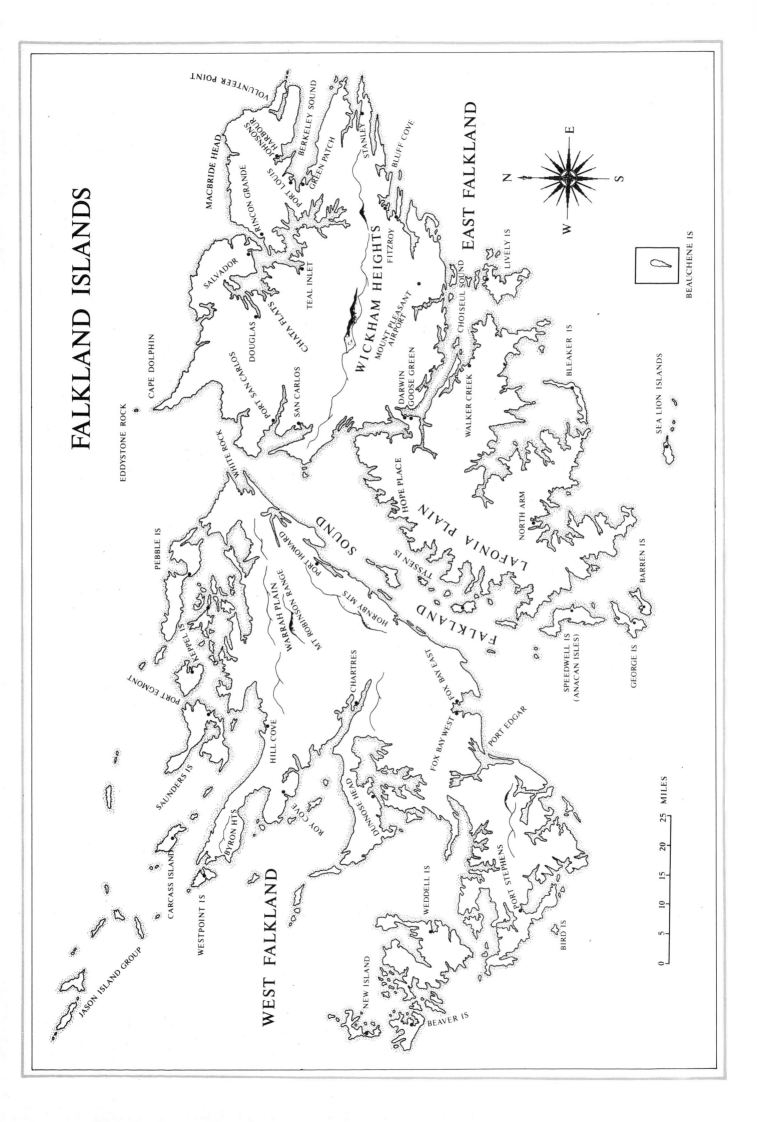

FALKLAND ISLANDS

EDDYSTONE ROCK

JASON ISLAND GROUP

CARCASS ISLAND
WESTPOINT IS
WEST FALKLAND
BYRON HTS
SAUNDERS IS
HILL COVE
ROY COVE
CHARTRES
DUNNOSE HEAD
NEW ISLAND
BEAVER IS
WEDDELL IS
BIRD IS
PORT STEPHENS
PORT EDGAR
FOX BAY WEST
FOX BAY EAST
KEPPEL IS
PORT EGMONT
PEBBLE IS
WHITE ROCK
WARRAH PLAIN
MT ROBINSON
PORT HOWARD
HORNBY MTS
WARRAH RANGE
SOUND
FALKLAND
TYSSEN IS
HOPE PLACE
SPEEDWELL IS
(ANACAN ISLES)
GEORGE IS
BARREN IS
NORTH ARM
LAFONIA PLAIN
WALKER CREEK
CAPE DOLPHIN
PORT SAN CARLOS
DOUGLAS
CHATA FLATS
SAN CARLOS
SALVADOR
RINCON GRANDE
MACBRIDE HEAD
JOHNSON'S HARBOUR
VOLUNTEER POINT
PORT LOUIS
BERKELEY SOUND
GREEN PATCH
STANLEY
BLUFF COVE
TEAL INLET
WICKHAM HEIGHTS
FITZROY
MOUNT PLEASANT AIRPORT
DARWIN
GOOSE GREEN
CHOISEUL SOUND
LIVELY IS
EAST FALKLAND
BLEAKER IS
SEA LION ISLANDS
BEAUCHENE IS

N
E
W
S

0   5   10   15   20   25   MILES

An Island schooner

In my travels around the Falkland archipelago I had come across many similar seabird colonies and, although not all were as large as this one, they contained many tens of thousands of birds. One of the most remarkable discoveries I made, however, was that so little seemed to be known, not only of their ecology but of their very existence.

When Charles Darwin wrote of his visit to the Falkland Islands more than 150 years ago he made no mention of such sights, describing the islands as appearing to be:

> an undulating land, with a desolate and wretched aspect, [which] is everywhere covered by a peaty soil and wiry grass, of a monotonous brown colour. Here and there a peak or ridge of grey quartz rock breaks through the smooth surface. Everyone has heard of the climate of these regions.

Practically all of Darwin's writings referring to the islands were in these sober tones, tones which were to be repeated by a succession of writers even though they may have had no first hand experience of them. So an image largely created by this authoritative naturalist has been handed down to become a traditional description.

Why Darwin was to cast this image we shall probably never know, although knowledge of the small area he visited and the fact that he made only two short visits to the islands, both in the austral autumn month of March, may possibly have influenced his writing. Darwin's travels took him to Port Louis, on the east coast of East Falkland mainland, and south along this coast to the area that now bears his name. Although there are many attractive areas in this region of the archipelago, Darwin's route took him over fairly flat moorland which in late

Wool production remains the main industry of the Islands

14

Capital town of Stanley, with Christ Church Cathedral

autumn, when browns are the dominant colours, may well have presented a 'desolate and wretched aspect', particularly in the unusually bad weather he experienced. Had Darwin ventured further, to other regions of the archipelago, he could not have failed to have written about these islands in more glowing terms.

This work is first and foremost about the natural beauty of this archipelago and for this reason it only takes the reader briefly through the history of the discovery and settlement of the islands. More emphasis has been placed on the history of those directly involved with the islands' environment – whalers, sealers and early colonists – for it is through their chronicles that we have a different and fascinating insight into the Falkland Islands and their natural history. The important message running through this book is that we are responsible for a very special, but extremely vulnerable and delicate, part of the world.

Writing about these islands, their environment, colour and feeling, is a challenge; one must feel all seasons, even smell and sample the flavour of the vastly different regions. The diversity of the landscape in the archipelago is so great that no one person could hope to explore it, let alone write in detail of its entirety. In my own quarter century of living in the Falklands I have used my own fascination for islands and natural life to travel and seek out new images in the archipelago, but this work can only touch on a small part of its total beauty and fascination. I hope it will be a challenge to all those who have written in sober tones of the Falkland Islands and present a new and improved view of a unique and beautiful group of islands.

Mixed colony of rockhopper penguins and black-browed albatross on remote outlier

16

1 The Islands are Discovered

I looked again, hardly believing it. But there amongst the mass of small pebbles and stones, was a perfect flint-stone spear head. The area where I had walked showed signs of erosion, small mounds of tussock peat dotted the headland, indicating that my find had conceivably been deposited there before a layer of vegetation and peat had hidden it. Now, perhaps hundreds of years later, it had come to light again.

The Falkland Islands lie only some 450km (300 miles) from the tip of South America and Cape Horn, the home of several indigenous Indian tribes which at one time lived on the shores of the intricate channels of that area and might well have reached these islands. The prevailing winds and currents continually deposit large quantities of debris on certain beaches in the Falklands. Much of this debris consists of the remains of false beech trees, species of *Nothofagus* which grow on the shores of the Magellan Straits. When the Yaghan Indians, the boat people of that region, still inhabited the straits, there were a number of records of Yaghan canoes being found on the beaches of the Falkland Islands. It seems very probable, therefore, that if wind and currents alone deposited empty canoes, the Indians may also have made the crossing, one of them perhaps the original owner of my spear head.

There is no evidence of any indigenous peoples being on the Falklands when voyagers from the northern hemisphere first sighted the group of islands, although in 1594 when Sir Richard Hawkins sailed along the northern part of the islands in the *Dainty* he made an intriguing comment in his writings: 'It was peopled. We saw many fires but could not come to speak with the people as we were in haste to shoot the Straites.' Hawkins may well have seen coastal tussock grass fires which are known to be caused by lightning but it is not impossible that he may also have witnessed the remnants of groups of Yaghans who could have landed and lived on the islands for a period in those earlier times.

Apart from the intriguing possibility of a group of Fuegian Indians having been the first to step ashore on these islands, exactly when the archipelago was first discovered by voyagers from elsewhere is still unclear and a point of discussion between historians.

Antoine Louis de Bougainville, the French navigator who established the first settlement in the islands, believed that the Florentine navigator Amerigo Vespucci made the first sighting in about 1502. There is also the possibility that one of Magellan's ships made the discovery, for maps prepared after his voyage in 1520 show islands off the Patagonian coast for the first time. These islands were to be called Islas de Sanson y de Patos, a reference to the many fat penguins that were found there. Another possibility is that one of Camargue's expeditionary vessels could have sighted the islands in 1540, for records from one of his ships mention sailing among islands described as 'bare with not a bit of woods, very windy and very cold and the prevailing winds are south-west, west and north-west and rarely are there other winds. In all this land there are many fowls, both from the land and sea and so too sea lions . . .' There are contradictions in these writings, but there is a view that the description does in fact refer to the Falkland Islands.

The hulk of the SS Great Britain before her restoration

In 1592 the British vessel *Desire*, commanded by John Davis, was parted from its companion and flagship the *Leicester*. John Jane, Davis' historian aboard the *Desire*, recorded:

> The ninth (August) wee had a sore storme, so that we were constrained to hull, for our sailes were not to induce any force. The 14th wee were driven in among certaine isles never before discovered by any known relation, lying fiftie leagues or better from the shore east and northerly from the Streights in which place, unless it had pleased God of his wonderful mercie to have ceased the winds, wee must of necessitie have perished.

The name Davis Southern Isles was thus given to the Falklands. Two years later, in 1594, Sir Richard Hawkins made his voyage, making his reference to the islands being 'peopled'. From his descriptions, Hawkins' first landfall would have been one of the outer Jason Islands, which he called Poynt Tremountaine. A little further on he passed Sedge Island, 'a low flat island of some two leagues long: we named it Fayre Island: for it was all over as greene and smooth as any meadow in the spring of the yeare'. Hawkins would have been referring to the tussock grass that covered this island, which from some distance offshore would have looked like a 'meadow'. Continuing his voyage round the north of the archipelago he came to the Falkland Sound,

> a goodly opening, as of a great river or an arme of the sea with a goodly low country adjacent. And eight or ten leagues from this opening, some three leagues from the shore lyeth a bigge rock, which at the first wee had thought to be a shippe under all her sayles.

Although many of Hawkins' quoted distances are not accurate in giving the relative positions of the points he described, there is little doubt that the 'bigge rock' which he named Condite-head is what we today call the Eddystone Rock.

Four years later, after this discovery of Hawkins Maiden Land, Dutchman Sebald de Weert commanding the *Gelaaf* also discovered the Jason Island group, which he called the Sebald Islands.

Other voyagers were to sight the islands but the first documented landing was not made until 1690 when the English vessel *Welfare* commanded by John Strong sailed to the South Atlantic on a voyage of discovery. An account of their visit to the islands leaves little doubt of the landing:

> The inhabitants, such as they were, were exceedingly numerous. The penguins gave us the first reception being mustered in infinite numbers on a rock. Upon some of our men landing, they stood, viewed and then seemed to salute them with a great many graceful bows, with the same gestures, equally expressing their curiosity and good breeding. As for other creatures, there were eagles, hawks which tho' they had long wings, suffered themselves to be taken by our men.

On his visit Strong sailed through the sound which divides the two main islands, which he named Falkland Sound after the then First Lord of the Admiralty. This was the first reference to the name Falkland. Eighteen years later, the name Falklands Land was given to the group by Captain Woode Rogers, an English privateer who sailed round the archipelago in 1708.

In 1701 the French navigator Jacques Gouin de Beauchene recorded a landing and discovered the island that still bears his name. For a number of years the French visited the islands with increasing frequency, calling them Iles Malouines. One young Frenchman particularly interested in the Malouines was the nobleman Antoine Louis de Bougainville. Bitter after the loss of Quebec and the cession of Canada to Britain, he viewed the prospects of a new colony in the Malouines as recompense for the blow struck at France. Preparing an expedi-

Mainmast of the SS Great Britain

Tower-like formations of quartzite on Grand Jason Island

tion in secret, de Bougainville left St Malo in September 1763 with two vessels, *Eagle* and *Sphinx*, bound for the islands. On their way south the little expedition called at Montevideo to load cattle, horses, pigs, goats, sheep and poultry for the new colony. On 31 January 1764 they sighted the Jason Island group and, following the coast to the east, came across 'la grande baye des Iles Malouines', known today as Berkeley Sound.

No other ship had sailed into this sound; what lay in store amidst the rolling landscape that now bordered their passage? If weather conditions were favourable, there would have been a cloudless sky, giving the sea a lovely blue-green cast, the surrounding hills an array of browns, reds and greys and the immediate coastline a rich green. The would-be settlers must have looked upon the islands with considerable excitement and expectations. Slowly feeling their way, the ships would have anchored at the head of what we now know as Berkeley Sound, perhaps in the lee of Long Island. From this anchorage a small boat would have pulled along the edge of the coast, through the narrow entrance and into the snug inner harbour or Careenage as it is known today. On 3 February 1764 a landing party inspected the new land.

Large flocks of birds flew over the landing party and ducks and geese walked the shores. Dom Pernety, botanist on the expedition, recorded that the land was covered with grass a foot or so high and that walking was difficult on account of the mounds of entangled roots and vegetation lying beneath the grass. The shores, Pernety noted, were covered with 'bullrushes and cornflags' which looked like small trees. Today there is little evidence of tussock grass on the shores of Berkeley Sound, but almost certainly this is what Pernety saw. The small boat party, which included de Bougainville and Pernety, made camp on the higher ground above a stream. Good water was plentiful, the land was covered with lush vegetation for the feeding of their stock and game was abundant.

Lord Anson in 1740 wrote of the potential importance of the archipelago and urged the Admiralty to claim the islands but an expedition was not launched until the year in which de Bougainville was settling on East Falkland. The expedition consisted of two ships, *Tamar* and *Dolphin*, under the command of Captain John Byron. On 15 January 1765 Byron entered the harbour which almost one year earlier de Bougainville had named Port de la Croizade. This was at Saunders Island, off the West Falkland. Byron named it Port Egmont in honour of the First Lord of the Admiralty and he claimed this and adjacent islands for George III in complete ignorance of de Bougainville's claim on behalf of France.

The *Tamar* and *Dolphin* continued their exploration and passed the entrance of the sound at the head of which lay the French settlement. Byron named this Berkeley Sound and had he entered would no doubt have discovered Fort St Louis. Byron's enthusiasm for the islands was shown in his reports. To the Admiralty he wrote:

> It has the greatest plenty of good water, and nothing wanting but wood. The soil is extremely good. Wild fowl of different kinds in such numbers that our people lived upon nothing else whilst we were there . . . the land is all covered with wood sorrel and wild sellery.

Shortly after Byron's expedition left rumours circulated in England that the French had already settled them and so in September 1765 an expeditionary force of three ships, the *Jason, Carcass* and *Experiment*, under Capt John McBride, sailed for the islands.

McBride's instructions were to inform any lawless person found on the islands that they were on land belonging to Great Britain. McBride arrived at Port Egmont on 8 January 1766 and there he started to set up a shore establishment in the form of a timber blockhouse which he had brought with him from England. McBride's reports did not show the same enthusiasm for the islands as Byron's. To Lord Egmont he wrote:

> Your Lordship will easily conceive what a dreary prospect a range of craggy barren mountains must afford, heightened by almost constant gales of wind . . . the numbers of sea lions, penguins and other vermin that are on and about these islands are incredible, which I suppose is the reason why there is such a scarcity of fish.

King cormorants stripping tussock grass stools of leaves for nest building

Shortly after his arrival in the islands, which he was to rename the Falkland Islands, McBride began to survey the western side of the archipelago, but this work stopped with the coming of the winter months. Not until late November of that year (1766), following the discovery by one of the survey parties of a stone cairn on a hill overlooking Berkely Sound, did McBride realise that they were

not the only human inhabitants. On 3 December the French settlement was sighted and on the following day McBride, aboard *Jason*, sailed up Berkeley Sound to Port Louis to view with some amazement ships, people, the small settlement and the fort belonging to the French. At the time of McBride's discovery Fort Louis was under the command of de Nerville, de Bougainville having returned to France. Although the French commandant rejected McBride's letter informing him of Britain's claims to the islands, the meeting was cordial and unofficially a great success. However, unknown to McBride and de Nerville, Spain had objected to the French settlement on islands which she already regarded as a dependency of her South American dominions, and de Bougainville had by that time agreed to transfer his new found colony to Spain.

Early in 1767 McBride returned to England to report, leaving Port Egmont under the command of Capt Rayner, shortly afterwards to be succeeded by Capt Hunt of the *Tamar*. At about the same time as McBride returned to England, a change in command was also taking place at Port Louis, little more than half a day's sailing from Port Egmont. On 1 April 1767 de Bougainville, now returned from France, and de Nerville formally handed over the French colony to Spain and the Spanish flag was raised over the little settlement which was renamed Port Soledad.

The Spanish governor, Felipe Ruiz Puente, his commander and his minister, did not have the same enthusiasm as the departing French colonists for their new possession. With the summer over and the days shortening with the approach of winter, they were not impressed. They complained of the state of the settlement:

> The buildings left behind by the French are not fit to be called houses, they are barracks . . . the dwelling left by the French commander M de Nerville is built of stone and chalk mixed with earth and is thatched with straw . . . it may be called a house, whereas the others, to the number of 36, are only huts, to be lived in in case of need.

and of the islands themselves: 'esta miserable tierra . . . todos los dias son nublados'. (This miserable land . . . every day is cloudy).

Although there is some question as to whether or not the Spanish knew where the British settlement was situated, the British certainly knew of Port Louis. Curiously, however, each ignored the existence of the other. Or was there another reason for this?

When the first American whalers commenced activities in the islands in about 1772 they referred to the West Falkland as the English Maloon and to East Falkland as the Spanish Maloon. Their maps of this period were so marked, indicating that they recognised two territories. Capt Charles Barnard, a whaler and sealer from Nantucket who chronicled his exploits about the islands in 1812–16, leaves little doubt of his understanding of two separate territories.

> While at anchor, in the month of April, in Fox Bay, on the SE side of the English Maloon, we described heavy columns of smoke rising in the direction of the Anacan Islands*, which are so low as not to be perceptible from where we were. (*viz. Eagle [now Speedwell], George and Barren islands [situated off the south of East Falkland]). Reflecting on this unusual appearance, I suspected that they arose from the fires of Spaniards, possibly from Buenos Ayres, on one of the Anacans, as I had often heard that the Spanish government was in the habit of sending out every year a Guarda Costa, to examine their harbours and passes for foreign vessels, and if any were found, to order them off immediately: and so apprehensive were they that the subjects of a foreign power might form even a temporary settlement, for the purpose of procuring seal skins

Deeply stratered coast typically used by fur seal; south west of West Falkland

and sea elephant's oil, that they often set fire to the tushooks, and thus destroyed the harbours of the seal, to prevent them as much as possible from resorting to these islands. I had almost resolved to go to the Anacans for seal, but as I could not banish the apprehension of falling into the hands of the Spaniards, I determined to remain at our present station until I should ascertain by whom these fires had been kindled.

We were now employed in examining the shores of the islands in the bay, in our pursuit of seal, of which we took several. As the columns of smoke continued to ascend in the same direction, I began to conjecture a variety of causes. Might they not proceed from hordes of the enemy, who might possibly use it as a decoy to secure us in their power? Did they arise from daring adventurers like ourselves, who were either preparing their food, or trying out the oil which they had collected? But such a supposition was improbable, as it is very rare that vessels touch at the Anacans.

Whether by design or not, confrontation between the British, now established at Port Egmont on Saunders Island and the Spaniards at Port Soledad, was not to come about for two and a half years. In September 1769 Capt Hunt, cruising in the *Tamar*, came across a Spanish schooner from Port Soledad. Hunt presented the master with a formal warning to leave the islands. Two days later *Tamar* on a surveying voyage on the coast of East Falkland was met by the schooner *San Felipe*. On board was a Spanish officer with a letter from the governor of Port Soledad giving Hunt formal notice to leave the islands. More letters passed between the governor of Port Soledad, Don Felipe Ruiz Puente, and Capt Hunt, each issuing notice to the other to leave. Spanish frigates were ordered to find the British settlement and force the occupants to leave. Finding this at first impossible, a larger force of five Spanish frigates were ordered to sail for the Islas Malvinas, as the Spanish called the islands. Although preparations were made for the defence of the Port Egmont shore establishment and shots were fired in retaliation, the British position was impossible and ended with the surrender of the settlement under articles of capitulation.

The two countries almost went to war over the episode but negotiations resulted in an order for restitution being signed on 7 February 1771. In September of that year, a British expedition returned to Port Egmont and the Spanish formally relinquished the settlement on 15 September 1771. Three years later the British withdrew the garrison from Port Egmont, an action which gave rise to speculation on what Britain's intentions were over the islands' future as a possession.

For the rest of that century and for part of the nineteenth century, Spain kept her settlement at Port Soledad. In spite of the efforts of one or two governors, the Spanish colony was never a great success and before the close of the eighteenth century the Spanish viceroy of Buenos Aires suggested that the settlement be abandoned.

In 1806 there were serious disturbances in Buenos Aires. With the news that the British had occupied that city, the Spanish governor at Port Soledad abandoned his post and fled to Montevideo. Four years later revolution resulted in Spain and her South American colonies parting, with jurisdiction over the Falklands being taken over by the newly formed United Provinces of the Rio de la Plata (later Argentina).

For a period of fourteen years, between 1806 and 1820, the islands were neglected by authority and became a haven for whalers and sealers. The abandoned Port Egmont, together with New Island, West Point Island and other harbours, became the self-styled homes of these men.

On 1 November 1820 the frigate *Heroina* commanded by Col Daniel Jewitt arrived at Port Soledad with instructions once again to take possession of the islands on behalf of the government of Argentina and on 6 November formal rights of possession were declared. On his arrival, Jewitt was to find some seventeen vessels, many being whaling or sealing vessels, and one of his first acts of authority was to send out a letter to masters forbidding whaling and sealing about the islands.

In 1823 an attempt at colonisation was made when a grant of land, with fishery and cattle rights on East Falkland was made by the Argentine government to Jorge Pacheco and Louis Vernet. This first attempt failed but in 1826 Vernet, determined to create 'a great national fishery' arrived with a second expedition. A merchant of Hamburg, French by birth but South American by naturalisation, Vernet hoped, no doubt, to continue where de Bougainville had commenced his small colony sixty years previously.

Between 1826 and 1831 Vernet established some ninety settlers, a cosmopolitan community of German, Dutch, Spanish, French, Portuguese and British. The community thrived and was prosperous and content, making a good living from the sale of produce. Salted fish was exported to Brazil and large quantities of dried beef sold to South America. Vegetables and fresh beef had a ready market with ships that called in at Port Soledad. In June 1828 Vernet was appointed governor of the Islas Malvinas, which immediately brought a protest from Great Britain and a claim to the islands being sent to the Minister of Foreign Affairs in Buenos Aires. But changes were already taking place in the islands which were to seal the course of events in the years to come.

Depredations by whalers and sealers of other nations had increased to such an extent that, on his appointment as governor on behalf of the Argentine government, Vernet issued a warning to masters of sealing and whaling vessels that unless they ceased operations they would be arrested. Few if any heeded the warning. In July 1831 Vernet seized the American sealer *Harriet* and took the vessel to Buenos Aires, where her master, Davison, was to stand trial. Davison escaped from custody in Buenos Aires and joined the American corvette *Lexington* which immediately set sail for Port Soledad, bent on retaliation for the loss of the *Harriet*. On 28 December 1831 the *Lexington* arrived at Soledad and on orders from her commander, Sylas Duncan, a force of men went ashore and sacked the settlement. The destruction of years of work by Duncan's action was a severe blow to Vernet but events that followed were to prevent him from ever returning and resurrecting his venture.

In September 1832 a temporary Argentine governor took over Port Soledad but his office came to an abrupt end shortly afterwards when he was attacked and killed by a group of mutineers from one of his vessels.

Perhaps prompted by the establishment of Vernet as governor of the Islas Malvinas and concern, following the *Lexington* episode, that the USA might have been contemplating the setting up of a naval base on the islands to protect their fisheries vessels, Britain decided to make a move. On 20 December 1832 there arrived at Port Egmont the *Clio* under Capt Onslow and the *Tyne* under Capt Hope, despatched from Great Britain to take possession of the islands. On 2 January 1833 they unexpectedly arrived at Port Soledad in order to issue to the commander there a letter to 'exercise the right of sovereignty over these Islands'. To Don Jose Maria Pinedo, then in charge of the settlement, this was, in his words, an insult. But perhaps after the death of his predecessor he was not sorry when on 5 January he was able to sail for Buenos

Aires aboard his vessel, the *Sarandi*. A few days later Capt Onslow departed in the *Clio*, leaving in temporary charge William Dickson, a British resident formerly employed as a storekeeper by Vernet.

In March 1833 the *Beagle*, commanded by Capt FitzRoy, called at the port, then renamed Port Louis. Charles Darwin was on board and both he and FitzRoy were dismayed at the state of the settlement, still in ruins after the actions of Sylas Duncan and his men. Of the inhabitants FitzRoy wrote: 'There are a handful of honest settlers, sealers and whalers of various nationalities, Indian convicts left by Vernet, *gauchos*, almost all wild, drifting from bad to worse'.

The handful of honest settlers to which he referred were William Low, William Dickson and Matthew Brisbane, the latter now being the senior British resident and in charge of Port Louis. Brisbane, who had been in charge of Vernet's fisheries and at the time of FitzRoy's visit was attempting to salvage the remains of that business, also tried to create law and order in the community. With the lawless element described by FitzRoy, Brisbane's task was to prove very difficult and ended in yet one more misfortune descending upon the settlement. The Indian convicts and *gauchos*, having tasted freedom, were unwilling to return to a lawful state. Plotting against Brisbane, five of the convicts and three *gauchos* took their chance and on 26 August 1833, when William Low and four of his men had left the settlement to go sealing, they attacked and murdered Brisbane, Dickson and three others. The remaining settlers, thirteen men, three women and two children, escaped to a nearby island where they remained until 23 October before being rescued by the sealing vessel *Hopeful* of London.

News of the murders did not reach London until December 1833. On 8 January 1834 HMS *Challenger* arrived at Port Louis. *Challenger* had previously been given orders to call at the Islands in order to land Lt Smith, who had been appointed naval superintendent of the Falkland Islands. On 10 January Smith was installed as superintendent and on the following day, anxious to put his new establishment right, he set off with a party of marines in search of the murderers. Of the original eight, five were eventually caught some weeks later, four being sent to England for trial. However, their arrest posed a problem, for under which law could they be tried? Eventually, after a term of imprisonment in Newgate, they were sent back to Montevideo as free men.

Once again the little settlement of Port Louis was faced with the task of rebuilding. The Indians and *gauchos* had left the settlement derelict. Tamed cattle and horses had been turned loose into the *camp* (from the Spanish *campos* meaning countryside) and gardens ruined. A resourceful person and, as Capt Grey of the *Cleopatra* described him, 'a man of about 45, active and from his appearance giving one a good idea of the healthiness of the climate', Lt Smith set out to repair and develop his establishment. Vernet, perhaps anxious to continue his business, wrote to Lt Smith offering advice: 'horses before houses'. Houses could be built at any time, Vernet wrote, but without horses cattle could not be brought in and without cattle, life could not exist.

A few of Vernet's original settlers remained, including three women. One of these was Antonina Roxa, who was held in high esteem by Smith. Following one of Vernet's recommendations particularly in regard to cattle taming, Lt Smith made an agreement with Antonina Roxa that, since he was unable to pay her for this work, she should have every other calf from every cow tamed for milking. This was the same system worked by Vernet with the German families he had had at Port Louis.

Under Smith the settlement thrived and when Capt Grey called at Port Louis in November 1836 to make a report on the state of the islands for the admiralty, he wrote of the settlement and its inhabitants:

> The principal house or cottage is that inhabited by Lt Smith and among the miserable huts by which it is surrounded looks respectable by comparison, it is white-washed, has a flagstaff before it and looks like some preventive station on the coast of Northumberland.
> A second cottage also cleanly white-washed is inhabited by the boats' crew. The country to the back of the settlement is common moorland covered with a sort of heather and coarse grass, and rises gradually towards the centre of the Island. There are the ruins of what had been probably barracks, situated in a hollow below the Governor's house. The actual number of inhabitants is at this moment eighteen and consists of Lt Smith, his son (an unpolished cub of 18), four or five of the boats' crew, an old Spanish gaucho, a French boy of 16, a most expert lad in every way, whether in a boat or on a horse, an American and three English deserters from merchant vessels, an old German who is by way of being a tailor and doctor of the establishment and three women who have been for some years on the Island. One of them is a Monte-Videan, half Indian, and is married to the American sailor, the other two are negroes, one the wife of old Coronel, and the other the widow of one of the other gauchos killed in the dispute I have related above; the widow has two young children.

and of their agricultural pursuits:

> I was astonished to find about two hundred head of tame cattle feeding on the adjoining hills, many of them cows with calves by their sides. The settlers had also a great supply of pigs, and also a very tolerable stock of poultry. Since we have been here the ship's company has been supplied with beef from the tame cattle, and the butter and milk we get is excellent, as good as any I have ever tasted at Hawick.

It was also reported that settlers who 'arrived without a sixpence in their pockets now possess two fine schooners and are making money rapidly.'

But it appears that much depended on who was in charge. The enthusiasm of Lt Smith was clear when on his return to England he wrote to a friend, G. T. Whitington:

> After living four years and a half on the Eastern Island so highly do I think of the islands that I would gladly take an active part in forming a colony and reside there with my family. The small settlement that now actually exists at Port Louis, East Falkland, though the inhabitants are there only on sufferance, without an inch of ground they can call their own, are thriving rapidly, which speaks volumes.

G. T. Whitington was probably the first to urge colonisation, having originally enquired about prospects in 1828 when Vernet was governor. Through an associate, Whitington had already obtained grants of land from Vernet. When Britain took possession, Whitington hoped that with the concessions he had obtained he could continue an establishment similar to Vernet's. He forwarded proposals to the British government but approval was not given; to have done so would have been recognition of Vernet's claim and indirectly that of the Buenos Aires government. Whitington continued to try to obtain rights without success. Finally he took a different course and in 1840 his brother, J. B. Whitington, set sail for the islands in an attempt, no doubt, to informally colonise, for shortly after his arrival he wrote to Lt Tyssen, then in charge of Port Louis, asking 'to be put in quiet possession of ten square miles'.

In that same year the Colonial Lands and Emigration Commissioners proposed that East Falkland be colonised and that Port Louis be the main town. On 2 August 1841 Richard C. Moody, at that time aged 28, was appointed in London as lieutenant governor and ordered to proceed to the islands to carry out the proposals.

When Moody arrived in early 1842 he brought with him a small group of new colonists. Although military personnel, a number were accompanied by their families and were to be the forerunners of a new colony. Moody's little party were not rural people but possessed skills as carpenters, masons, smithies, surveyors and bricklayers. At first they must have relied greatly on the skills of some of those described by Grey, people who by necessity had learnt to survive on what was around them such as the wild cattle and game.

Other immigrants were to follow Moody, and shortly after his arrival he reported having been joined by a sheep farmer from Lincolnshire together with his family and stock. Later he referred to a few Scottish settlers and 'how well fitted they are to these parts'.

Moody's reports leave little doubt that he was impressed with the islands. He had great hopes for their future and their capacity to survive on their own natural resources. He made many sound suggestions which, had he been able to implement them, would have benefitted the islands today. Moody had great hopes for a new town to be laid out at Port Louis. Anson, as he proposed naming it, would be the temporary principal town, awaiting the growth of colonisation before any decision was taken on building another town elsewhere. The Lands and Emigration Commission, however, had other ideas, expressing their opinion to Lord Stanley, then Secretary of State for the Colonies, that 'the site of the capital should be fixed at whichever port should be decided by competent authority to offer the greatest advantage to shipping'.

Drury Street, Stanley, and original Pensioners' Cottages

Some four years before Moody's arrival in the islands Lt Sulivan had surveyed the waters of Port William, lying a few miles to the south of Berkeley Sound and Port Louis. This survey had found Port William and an inner harbour known as Jackson's Harbour to be better for shipping than Port Louis. Shortly after Moody had arrived to take up his duties at Port Louis, he was instructed by Lord Stanley to investigate Port William as a new town site. From a landsman's point of view, it appears that Moody was not convinced about the suitability of such a site and after inspecting the area again at the onset of winter, he reported to Lord Stanley that he was concerned about the wet state of the land at Port William.

At the time of this inspection, the Ross Antarctic Expedition was anchored at Port Louis. Moody sought Capt Ross's advice on the selection of Port William as the new town site and in the midwinter month of June 1842 Moody and Ross, accompanied by Capt Crozier and Lt Sulivan, inspected the area. Four sites were chosen, two positions on the coast of Port William and two on the south side of Jackson's Harbour. Moody still had reservations about the suitability of the land although on the credit side he reported it had vast deposits of peat, estimated as covering 126 sq km (56 sq miles).

Capt Ross, as the competent authority, reported on the advantages to shipping of Port William and in March 1843 Lord Stanley wrote to Moody: 'You will therefore take the necessary steps for removing to that place (Port William) as early as possible'.

In July 1843 work began on the new town site, Moody having selected a north facing slope on the southern shore of Jackson's Harbour. A year later, after what proved to be a slow and arduous move from Port Louis, Moody wrote to Lord Stanley suggesting the new capital bear the name of the Secretary of State. Officially the town of Stanley came into being on 18 July 1845, Jackson's Harbour being renamed Port Stanley.

Today Stanley remains as the capital town of the Falkland Islands, the administrative centre for the islands' wool industry and still the main port. The town itself, set out along a sloping hillside overlooking Stanley Harbour, lies as Moody planned, a series of parallel roads running the length of the north facing slope of the hillside, with intersecting roads running at right angles from the top of the slope down to the harbour front. The houses, all with their own garden plot, lie in formation along the roads with almost military precision. All face north to take full advantage of the sun. On days of intense sunlight the coloured iron roofs of the little town present a bright patchwork appearance, a vivid splash of colour against the subtle greys, greens and buffs of the surrounding landscape.

To many visitors, Stanley presents the only image of the Falkland Islands, but it is outside the precincts of the capital in the *camp*, or countryside, where a unique environment, a land of islands, coasts, mountains and plains, presents the true image of these islands.

Standing on a vantage point, perhaps 15m (50ft) above the shoreline, a wide expanse of sand curls away ahead of me for over a mile before being interrupted by a rocky headland. The beach, typical of many found over the archipelago, is a dazzling white from the wind polished quartzite particles which make up the accumulation. Such is the reflective power of this quartz (silica) sand that in conditions of strong light it is painful to the eyes to walk on such beaches.

2 The Coastal Regions

There is an offshore wind which, as the surf rolls in to make its final break on shore, lifts white plumes of spray in an apparent effort to throw back the surf. At times the surf presents a wall of clear blue water and every now and again a small pod of dolphins race the length of the curling wall of water, giving a unique underwater view of these graceful animals.

A short distance offshore the colour of the sea is broken by irregular streaks of golden brown, marking beds of *Macrocystis*, the species of kelp which grows in the deeper offshore water. It is a colourful spectacle, the deep blue-green of the sea, the golden brown kelp, white beach and a brilliant blue sky as a backcloth.

From my vantage point I have been watching the progress of a group of gentoo penguins as they porpoise through the sea towards the shore, but several times when I thought they would make their final approach through the surf, they would hesitate and turn out to sea again. I wondered if the presence of the dolphins worried them but then I spotted what concerned them. Moving very slowly through the water parallel to the beach was the hardly definable shadow of a sea lion. Very occasionally it broke the surface, revealing only the blunt nose and forehead of an old male animal. Now I knew why the birds were concerned, for it is very often that these seal prey on penguins. Why these animals, which normally feed on squid and octopus, turn to preying on penguins may always remain a mystery; although it is no coincidence that in nearly all cases it is the old bull seals seemingly unattached to a colony that follow this pursuit.

What interested me was how the birds appeared to know the animal was there. As far as I could see there had been no visual contact – or could the penguins have sensed the seal's presence by sound? Once again the penguins were heading inland but I had lost sight of the seal. Suddenly there was a heave in the water some little distance from the birds. The next instant the group of gentoos were circling in disarray. Seconds later a penguin leapt high out of the water followed by the glistening body of the seal; for another moment nothing, then the head of the sea lion appeared dragging up out of the water the dark and silver-white form of a gentoo penguin. The seal had the penguin by its neck, the bird's head inside its mouth. With one enormous sideways thrust of its own head, the seal slapped the body of the penguin on the water's surface. This movement was carried out several times, the bird appearing to disintegrate. Already, seemingly out of nowhere, groups of dominican gulls, dolphin gulls and giant petrels were scavenging, fighting amongst themselves for morsels of the seal's prey. Apparently now disinterested in the penguins, the seal disappeared. Later the sea was to cast up the remains of the gentoo, a perfectly

The coast of Port Stephens, West Falkland, from Bird Island

Tidal pool with (Lessonia sp) of kelp

Kelp seaweed (Macrocystis pyrifera) growing offshore in deeper waters

Colony of dolphin gulls

Sand grass

intact skeleton and attached at the feet, like a glove being peeled off the hand, the equally intact skin, the whole now picked clean by the scavenging birds. Many times I have come across remains at different sites, all bearing the same pattern but rarely with signs indicating that the seals have attempted to eat their prey.

A group of gentoos were now coming ashore, their silver-white plumage wet and glistening in the sun as they plummeted out of the surf. Then, flippers flailing in order to gain their feet, they ran up the beach well clear of the water. Like sentinels, several hundreds of these birds are standing on the upper reaches of the tideline, preening and drying themselves, apparently calm and undisturbed by the drama which had taken place in the water before them. The newcomers join the group and also start to preen. At the same time a number of birds further up the beach detach themselves from the main group and begin to make their way inland.

With flippers outstretched and slightly back to assist their balance they stride out inland towards a clay slope that leads up into a shallow valley. For a short period only their heads are visible as they make their way between large patches of sea cabbage (*Senecio candicans*) their bright orange bills contrasting with the silvery grey of the plant's foliage; then they disappear from view as

Gentoo and rockhopper penguins coming ashore

*Group of incubating
king penguins with
gentoo penguins,
north coast of East
Falkland*

they follow a well worn track up the slope. So frequently has this route been used over the years that it is now in the form of a trench through the clay, deeper than the height of the penguins themselves. At the top of the clay slope the track widens and fans out to form what can only be described as one of nature's bowling greens. It is many yards wide and stretches out like a long green finger up the valley. Every few hundred yards this finger spreads out into roughly circular greens of larger expanses of fine grasses, then continues inland.

The party of gentoo penguins continues its journey following the path of green grass. Against the bright green are splashes of white and pink coloured excreta marking the passage of birds and helping the eye to follow the route up and down the rolling contours of the valley. In the far distance, over a mile from the beach, two other small groups of penguins can be seen moving against the horizon, one moving further inland, the other heading towards the sea.

Away from the rich green turf, the vegetation is a complex mixture of ground-hugging shrubs, ferns, coarse grasses and other plants, although a quick cast of one's eye over the landscape does show that the dominant vegetation is made up of a coarse, rather sober coloured grass known as white grass (*Cortaderia pilosa*). It is interspersed with a darker coloured shrub known as diddle-dee (*Empetrum rubrum*) and occasional patches of the small fern (*Blechnum penna marina*) and brown swamp rush (*Rostkovia magellanica*).

It is evident from the continual passage of these penguins that they have

*Pages 38–9:
The North coast of
East Falkland,
looking west to
Campa Menta*

been largely instrumental in the creation of the paths of fine green grass. But what of the larger areas? Following the birds up the valley and over a small rise, I could hear the clamour of many birds. Some little distance away perhaps a thousand birds clutter a small flat plain. Amongst the diddle-dee shrubs, ferns and other plants, the birds are moving around forming nests from this vegetation. Some birds are sitting on huge piles of woody stem, pieces of fern and grass, occasionally stretching out their necks to pull at a piece of vegetation protruding from the churned-up ground. It is the month of October, the austral spring, and the birds are beginning their breeding season on a new site.

A short distance back on the coastal side of this new nesting ground is a large area devoid of vegetation, the peaty ground black and compacted. The remains of a few nests, the quill-like tail feathers of gentoos and the odd piece of egg shell identify last year's site. Still further back along the penguins' route is another area, the nest site of two years ago, but hardly identifiable as such for it has been recolonised by vegetation. Instead of shrubs, fern and coarse grasses, however, the area is covered with patches of groundsel and tufts of finer grasses. And so the picture is complete. Generally the penguins will move each season to obtain nest material; in doing so the new site is stripped of vegetation, churned up and fertilised by the birds' rich guano. The original vegetation is usually destroyed completely and the enriched soil provides the right conditions for the finer grasses to establish. It is puzzling that groundsel commonly colonises these nest sites initially for the plant is not prolific elsewhere in the islands. I have often wondered if the seeds may be carried on the oceans' currents and are ingested by the penguins while they feed at sea.

Page 42 (top):
Kelp seaweed
(Durvillea antarctica)
exposed at low tide

(Below)
Algae growing on
storm beach boulders

Page 43 (top)
Short-eared owl (Asio
flammeus) *sheltering*
in tussock grass

(Below)
Bull elephant seal
(Mirounga leonina)
lying in a bed of
Durvillea *kelp*

Young male elephant
seals sparring.
Volunteer Lagoon

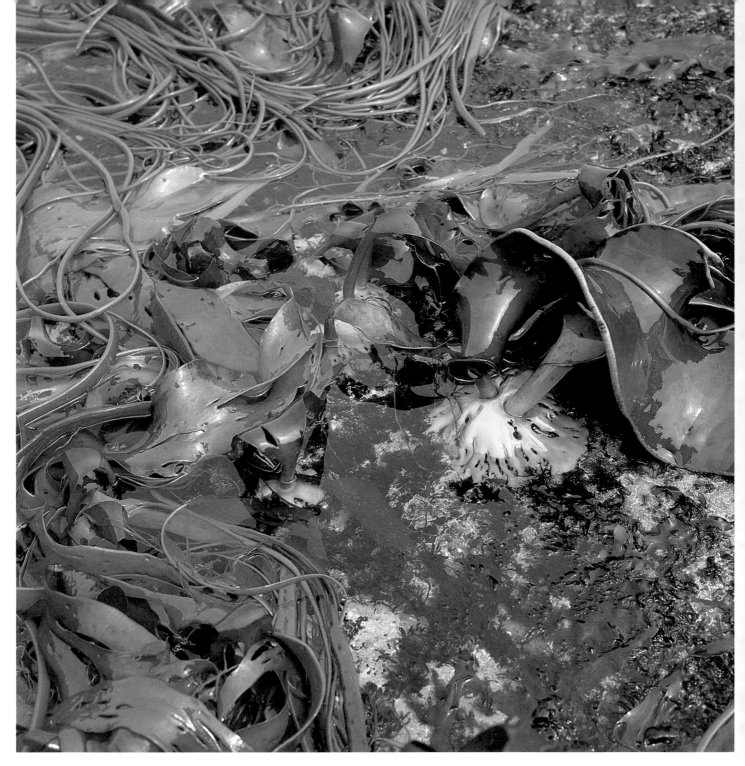

*Volunteer Beach,
north coast of East
Falkland*

It is not clear why these penguins tend to progress inland when establishing new nest sites. I came across one of the most interesting examples of this progression at a site on the north coast of East Falkland. Over a number of years, the birds on the south side of Volunteer Point have progressed inland to a site on a low hill some three miles from their landing place. The birds entered and left by the same route, making a round trip of six miles. Having reached the higher elevation the penguins called a halt to their progression; with the new site having a commanding view of both sides of the peninsula. The birds then established a second route to the north and the open sea, a distance of only one and a half miles. Strangely, they used the new route as an exit only, still entering the colony by the longer, original path.

Volunteer Point is a large peninsula, its north-eastern shores open to the South Atlantic, its opposite coast embraced by a large tidal lagoon. At the mainland end of the peninsula the lagoon sweeps round to meet a narrow isthmus which joins the point to the mainland. At the other end of the peninsula, the lagoon breaks out into the open sea through a narrow entrance in a sandbar. It is probable that many thousands of years ago the isthmus too was no more than a sandbar or barrier beach with the sea running through, and the peninsula effectively an island. Then, perhaps starting with an exceptional storm, this entrance was closed and gradually an isthmus was formed from the barrier beach. Today the isthmus, perhaps 6m (20ft) above sea level, forms one huge green. Although not the direct result of gentoo penguins, other bird life will have played an important part in the formation of this fertile ground.

On these open coasts, heavy winter seas pile the beaches high with kelp torn away from holdfasts or anchorages on the bottom of the sea. Gradually these piles are covered with sand and rot away, or become fermenting baths for elephant seal during their moult. A fertile base developed over centuries and the isthmus, at one time an infertile beach, became colonised by plants. A new habitat formed and the area eventually became a breeding ground for gulls, terns, oyster-catchers, and perhaps gentoos. All contribute to the fertility of the area and plant life advances. Grasses then develop and the grazing species of bird begin to play their part, one that has continued until the present.

Pages 46–7:
The peaks of Steeple
Jason from Grand
Jason

Large numbers of upland and ruddy-headed geese graze along the green. There are sheep also, but this is a scene which existed long before man introduced his stock. Spread evenly over the finely cropped grass are the droppings of geese, effectively replacing much of what they have grazed. Other birds add nutrients and even the sea continues to play a major part. In the winter, when the growth of the grass slows down, the whole green becomes covered with a top dressing of sand, which adds nutrients and contributes to the build-up of the isthmus. Perhaps one day an exceptionally heavy sea will throw up a barrier across the present narrow entrance of the lagoon and another isthmus will start to build up.

A few miles further up the East Falkland coast from Volunteer Point, another large sand beach, known as Cow Bay, presents a truly spectacular silver white expanse of quartz sand. Lying behind this 1.5km (1 mile) long beach is an area of water known as Loch Head Pond. Although varying from 137 to 1,207m (150 to 1,320yd) in width, this water winds inland some 4.3–6km (3.5–4 miles), the largest pond or lake in the islands. The waterway is also unique in other ways: it is brackish and differs from other ponds in its formation, having steep sloping sides and deep waters. Most interesting of all is that the waters hold a form of mullet, evidence that at one time this was a seaway. In the same way that Volunteer Point beach probably created a barrier and isthmus, Cow Bay beach was thrown up to dam Loch Head waters, trapping a large volume of sea water and marine life behind it.

Large numbers of freshwater ponds dot the landscape of the islands. Many are small, formed by simple depressions in the peat or clay topsoils and, where

they are isolated on ridges or on the tops of peat banks, are often devoid of plant and animal life.

In some areas, notably on the northern coastal areas of East Falkland, the *camp* is potmarked with thousands of miniature pools. Locally known as *soft camp*, the underlying ground is soft black peat where the water table rises to just below the surface. Between the pools, and forming a firm mat of rigid dark green leaves, grows *Astelia pumila*. Even in midwinter when the water table rises and the carpet of vegetation between these pools is also saturated, the *Astelia* produces a hard firm surface on which to walk. But, place a foot wrong and you could sink to the knee in the soft peat. These pools, in which the water is stationary and derived from rains and a rising water table, are also largely devoid of animal life. In complete contrast to these lifeless stands of water are ponds which are teeming with life.

Many such ponds are situated in the coastal areas, often on the coastal greens or in valleys where they may be fed by streams or springs. Here the level of fertility appears to have built up, influenced by their close proximity to a rich marine environment or by fresh water sources continually restocking with nutrients. Many of these ponds support dense growths of aquatic plants such as water milfoil (*Myriophyllum elatinoides*), or extensive beds of spike rush (*Eleocharis melanostachys*). Such areas are a haven for a variety of bird life. Grebes frequent such weedy ponds, building nests in the dense cover of rush. The small yellow-billed teal is also common to these ponds. I have come across breeding pairs on ponds only a few yards in diameter, the birds apparently subsisting well on the rich food matter which is deposited by streams. Most of these freshwater ponds are shallow, with vertically cut banks topped with a rich green sward of fine grass. Upland and ruddy-headed geese are to be found grazing these areas, while in the mid-summer and austral autumn large numbers congregate on certain ponds to moult.

In contrast to the wide expanses of silver white sand beaches, many of the north coast beaches on East Falkland are small, often steeply sloping, shingle beaches of highly polished pebbles of quartzite with a small percentage of agate. Although much of this coastline has a very similar pattern, cliffs rarely rising more than 15m (50ft) above the sea, sharply cut and flat topped, it presents some of the most interesting and attractive landscape in the Falklands. A mass of small coves, points and headlands, every one presenting a different vista, continues for some 90km (60 miles) from Volunteer Point to Cape Dolphin broken occasionally by sweeping sand beaches.

When Dr Hooker visited the islands in 1842 he walked part of the coastline and described some of the vegetation:

> During early spring the banks near the sea are enamelled with a few highly beautiful and conspicuous flowers, such as are chiefly common to Patagonia: they are *Oxalis enneaphylla*, a wood-sorrel, with blossoms larger than those of the snowdrop; a curious little *Calceolaria*, bearing a single large flower; a yellow violet; and a *Sisyrinchium*, which with the common *European Cerastium arvense*, whiten the clay-slate banks that skirt the shores of Berkeley Sound.

Of other plants along the coast, Hooker recorded:

> Nowhere in the world are *Lichens* more conspicuous than in the Falklands. The beautiful *Usnea melaxantha*, also a native of the arctic regions, forms a miniature shrubbery on the tops of naked rocks on the hills; while their sides are coated with many species, almost invariably identical with those of Great Britain. Along the sea

Cape Pembroke lighthouse

beach grow many species of this group, especially a pendent Ramalina, very near the *R.scopulorum* of Europe, and attaining a length of eight inches: it hangs so copiously from the rocks as in many places to cover them entirely.

Sea-weeds abound prodigiously on the outer rocky coasts, nor did we elsewhere see such enormous masses of marine vegetation as were cast upon the beach of the east shore of the Falklands. They consist principally of *Macrocystis pyrifera*, mentioned as a native of Kerguelen's Land, *Lessoniae* and *D'Urvillea utilis*. Wrenched from their attachment to the rocks and washed ashore, these sea-weeds become twisted together by rolling in the heavy surf, till they form enormous vegetable cables, much thicker than the human body, and several hundred feet in length. In some parts, the beach is so cumbered with these masses that walking becomes quite laborious; the pedestrian sinks frequently to the knees in the decaying heaps, and animal substance being also caught up, as in a net, the traveller's progress is rendered both offensive and tedious. Many most rare and beautiful sea-weeds may be detected here, either torn from inaccessible rocks far out to sea with the larger kinds, or growing parasitically upon them . . .

One gigantic genus is particularly abundant in the seas near the Falklands and Cape Horn, and surpasses all others in bulk. It is called *Lessonia* (after the naturalist of Captain Duperrey's expedition) and altogether resembles a tree in its mode of growth. The stem or trunk attaches itself by clasping fibres to the rocks, always beyond high-water mark: it attains a height of eight or ten feet and the thickness of a man's thigh: it branches upwards; and the ends of the branches give out leaves two or three feet long, and barely three inches broad, which, when in the water, hang down like the boughs of a willow. In many places the plant is so copious that it forms a submerged forest. On looking down from a boat through the transparent water where it grows, nothing but a mass of green foliage can be seen. There are several different species of this sea-weed, all attaining great size. The stems, when washed on shore, bear such an exact resemblance to dead wood as quite to deceive the eye: no arguments of mine could dissuade the captain of a merchant brig, with whom I visited a portion of the Falkland Islands, from taking several boat-loads on board his vessel: he was perfectly convinced that this sea-weed would afford, when dried, excellent fuel. A better use is made of it by the Gauchos, who shape pieces of the stem into knife-handles; when moist they drive the base of the blade into it, and leaving it to dry, it becomes harder than horn, and no force can sever the instrument from this novel kind of haft.

Today the banks along this northerly coastline of East Falkland can still be a profusion of wild flowers, the coast cliffs covered with lichens and the beaches a mass of kelp. But with the development of the islands' sheep industry significant changes in the vegetation have taken place. Hooker described vividly the coastal stands of tussock grass of East Falkland, a description which sadly does not fit the scene today:

> The peculiar mode of growth of the Tussock-grass enables it to thrive in pure sand, and near the sea, where it has the benefit of an atmosphere loaded with moisture, of soil enriched by decaying sea-weeds, of manure, which is composed in the Falkland Islands of an abundant supply of animal matter, in the form of guano, and of the excrements of numerous birds, who deposit their eggs, rear their young, and find a habitation amongst the groves of Tussock. Its general locality is on the edges of those peat bogs which approach the shore, where it contributes considerably to the formation of peat. Though not universal along the coast of these islands, the quantity is still prodigious, for it is always a gregarious grass, extending in patches sometimes for nearly a mile, but seldom seen, except within the influence of the sea air.

At the time of Hooker's visit to the islands, Governor Moody also reported on this grass, making some interesting comments on its agricultural value and also of the need to conserve the tussock (*Poa flabellata*):

> During several long rides into the country, I have always found the Tussock flourishing most vigorously in spots exposed to the sea, and on soil unfit for any other plant, *viz.* the rankest peat bog, black or red. It is wonderful to observe the beaten footpaths of the

Shepherd, East Falkland

wild cattle and horses, marked like a foot-track across fields in England, extending for miles over barren moor land, but always terminating in some point or peninsula covered with this favourite fodder, amid which one is almost certain to meet with solitary old bulls, or perhaps a herd of cattle; very likely, a troop of wild horses, just trotting off as they scent the coming stranger from afar. To cultivate the Tussock-grass, I should recommend that its seed be sown in patches, just below the surface of the earth, and at distances of about two feet apart; it must afterwards be weeded out, for it grows very luxuriantly, frequently attaining a height of six or seven feet. It should not be grazed, but cut or reaped in bundles. If cut, it quickly shoots again, but it is much injured by grazing; for all animals, especially pigs, tear it up, to get at the sweet nutty-flavoured roots. I have not tried how it would be relished if made into hay, but cattle will eat the dry thatch off the roof of a house in winter; their preference to Tussock-grass being so great, that they scent it a considerable distance, and use every effort to get at it. Some bundles, which had been stacked in the yard at the back of Government House, were quickly detected, and the cattle in the village made, every night, repeated attempts to reach them.

Moody clearly realised the potential of tussock grass as a fodder and in a letter to Lord Stanley he wrote:

> Enclosing and improving tracts of tussock grass on the coasts for winter fodder. This is very admirable and ought to be commenced as early as possible. The value of this fodder is only to be conceived by those who have witnessed the fondness which cattle show for it and have tasted the beef so fed.

Very few stands of tussock remain on the main islands today. In parts, finer grasses have taken the place of these stands, but in other areas distorted mounds of fibrous matter standing on acres of black peaty ground are all that remain of the tussocks. With the action of wind and rain they change in shape from year to year growing smaller as erosion continues. The remains of burrows where petrels once bred can be seen in many of these old tussock stools. Where erosion has gone further, clay subsoil stands stark against the landscape, the only evidence of the bird and animal life that used the tussock as a habitat being small mounds of smooth rounded pebbles, a feature of many penguin sites, and the occasional group of seal bones.

Hooker wrote of the ecology of the grass:

> The Tussock in its native state seems of almost no service in the animal economy. A little insect, and only one that I observed, depends on it for sustenance; and a bird, no bigger than a sparrow, robs it of its seeds; a few sea-fowl build amongst the shelter of its leaves; penguins and petrels seek hiding places amongst the roots, because these are soft and easily penetrated; and sea-lions cower beneath its luxuriant foliage; still, except the insect, I know no animal or plant whose extinction could follow the absence of this, the largest vegetable production in the Falklands, which does not support even a parasitical fungus. These same sea birds breed and burrow where no Tussock grows; rocks, elsewhere, suit the sea-lion's habits equally well; and the sparrow, which subsists on other food eleven months of the year, could surely make shift without this for a twelfth.

Were Hooker able to walk the same coasts today and view the eroding petrel burrows, long since vacated by these birds and the absence of many other species of bird, he would write of the importance of the grass as a habitat in very different tones.

Some of the largest concentrations of Magellan penguins found in the islands are situated along the north coast of East Falkland. Mile after mile of coast green is pitted by thousands of their nest burrows, this penguin being the only Falkland species which makes an underground nest chamber.

52

Breeding elephant seals on East Falkland

In the austral spring month of September these migratory penguins make their return to the islands' shores to begin breeding. Incredibly, the birds appear on almost the same day every year. One mid September on a deserted beach I watched one lone Magellan penguin make its way ashore and through a maze of still empty burrows. With almost no hesitation the bird made its way to one of the thousands of burrows. The following day it was busy cleaning out its old breeding site, which it had not visited for some five or six months. That day I watched the next arrivals and within a day or two, thousands more were re-occupying their burrows. In early morning and late evening the braying call of Magellan penguins echoes over the coastal landscape, a haunting melody which is part of the Falklands coastal scene much as the call of the curlew is part of some English coastal marshes.

About the same time as the Magellan penguins return to their breeding grounds, elephant seal also appear on the islands' coasts to breed. For me, their return heralds spring and the start of another breeding season on the islands. Day and night the low rumbling calls of males holding territories float across the coastal areas. The calls of these huge seal have an amazing carrying capability and on still, damp evenings their low throaty calls can be heard several miles away. Following the males, the females come ashore to pup and soon the male calls are joined by the higher pitched lamenting calls of females and the

53

yelping of their pups, so like the barking of a small dog that my first experience of these creatures had me looking for a dog, as I thought, lost in the *camp*!

Unlike the sea lion and fur seal, which are capable of using their fore and hind limbs for a form of walking and climbing, the elephant seal, belonging to the group of true seals (the *Phocidae*) does not have the same agility on land. It relies largely on its body muscles for movement. Although seemingly rather ungainly, their forward movement is almost fluid with their sleek cigar-shaped bodies rippling as they move. Due to their restricted movement on land, elephant seal favour the more gradually inclined beaches composed of sand or shingle on which to haul up and breed. On the West Falkland mainland they are less abundant, perhaps owing to the general lack of more suitable beaches.

Between the main islands of East Falkland and West Falkland lies the Falkland Sound. From its northern entrance to its opening at the south lies a stretch of water approximately 75km (50 miles) in length and with an average width of about 15km (10 miles). More than two thirds of the south-east shore of the sound is bordered by the East Falkland's large flat plain of Lafonia. Much of this shoreline is flat, rising only a few feet above sea level, with gradual shelving beaches. Following a similar pattern, the majority of the offshore islands in the sound are also flat and low lying.

On the west side of the Falkland Sound the shores of West Falkland, in complete contrast to the East Falkland side, present a very different coastal landscape. From White Rock Bay, the northern end of this coast, to the southern extremity of Fox Bay, the coastline is marked by a rocky ridge. Maintaining an even height of some 152m (500ft) throughout its 75km (50 mile) length, the ridge presents a most unusual scene. Like some giant causeway or bank heaped up to protect the eastern shore of the West Falkland island from the sound, it runs its entire length in an incredibly straight line. In geological terms the ridge follows the trend of the folded quartzites which present the principal mountain ranges sweeping from east to west across both main islands and, in the case of this ridge, parallel with the Falkland Sound. In parts the ridge is cut through, forming narrow entrances into well protected harbours behind the ridge. One of the most interesting of these is Port Edgar, at the southern end of the ridge.

In 1836 Capt Grey, engaged in a survey of the islands, described this harbour:

> Port Edgar being drawn as a very large harbour in the chart and from being named after the surveyor, I expected to be a good anchorage for the ship. Captain Stone of the *Eveline* could give me no information about this place and told me he had never been there and it was not frequented by the Sealers.
>
> I had found Edgar's chart so very incorrect that I could not trust to that, but with a good look out for the patches of kelp and with the boat leading the way I determined to run the risk. Besides the wind had freshened to a very strong breeze and in case of not finding an anchorage, I should be obliged to stand out to sea for the night, which would probably delay me a day or two in recording the line I was making round the Islands.
>
> For some time while running along this unbroken cliff I could see nothing like the entrance of a harbour and when I did discover it it had at first only the appearance of a ravine or a long cleft in the rock; the ship was signalised to heave to, to examine this entrance.
>
> The cliff was a wall on each side of it, from side to side it was only 195 ft, standing on a ledge of the rock, which was so perpendicular that one could hardly find a footing, I dropped the lead into the water and found seven fathoms (36 ft) deepening almost immediately in mid-channel to fourteen fathoms, and the opposite side was equally steep, the narrow length of the passage was about 400 yards and beyond a magnificent bay which forms by many degrees the finest harbour I have ever seen in my life.

Typical coast formation of the south west of West Falkland

54

I, of course, did not hesitate in making signal for the ship to run in and it was a beautiful sight as she foamed in between those abrupt rocks which appeared almost to overhang her decks. She was going about ten knots and passing us in the narrow passage threw such a spray into the boat that we were all soaked. Leardet told me afterwards that running through this ravine would have been a most nervous affair to all on board had it not been for my signal, finding that although the ship hove to for me inside that I should have difficulty in getting on board, I signalised to them to anchor as convenient and followed over towards the opposite side, near which, at the mouth of a creek, Mr Fittock picked up a capital berth for the ship; while they were furling the sails and moving the ship I landed in the creek and hardly had put my foot on shore, when one of the foxes of the country was chased by Pilot, I ran up as they were fighting and came to the poor dog's assistance who had nearly met his match, and a rifle ball soon settled the business, but Pilot had received a terrible bite in the leg.

I had heard that there were a great number of these foxes, but I had not seen one before, they are supposed to be indigenous to the Island, they are much larger than the English fox and not quite so large as a wolf. In shape they resemble a fox, their colour is much darker than that of our foxes, and the fur thicker; they are also longer in proportion in the legs, they are called here "Warrahs" or "Wolf Fox", the one I had killed was a very old one and I never saw such teeth.

*Remote offshore
tussock island*

Grey also wrote:

> Monday, December 19. Starting this morning early with the gig in company and intend-
> ing to return to the ship in time for the boats' crew dinner, Mr Fittock and myself pro-
> ceeded to examine Port Edgar, we found several creeks all of which had runs of water
> . . .
>
>   Although both wind and tide would be against us to return, yet so interested was I to
> discover the end of this extraordinary channel, that I ran on although we had none of
> our tent apparatus in the boat, at last we opened out into an immense lake, which
> extended in a basin as far nearly as we could see with numbers of small islands covered
> with tussock, the banks of the channel had been steep and rugged, here the land was
> quite low at the shores and rose gradually with a gentle slope towards the hills; in the
> background so far as one could see there was nothing to break the eye, all was moorland
> and covered with heather and coarse brown grass, the sands were covered with birds of
> all descriptions and as the boat sailed past the bays these birds did not move, the report
> of a rifle sent them all screaming into the air for a minute or two but they settled again
> almost immediately.

Grey's account of the foxes is interesting in that it is one of the few first-hand accounts of these creatures. The first description of this wolf-like fox was given by Simson who sailed with Capt Strong in the *Welfare* in 1689–90. He described the animal as a fox twice the size of the English species. De Bougainville referred to the animal as *loup-renard* while Capt Byron, who found a number on West Falkland and from them named Fox Bay, noted them as being as big as middle-sized mastiffs which, according to his men, 'were creatures of great fierceness resembling wolves'. The early settlers on East Falkland, however, appear to have found them timid creatures. Governor Moody wrote of the Warrah or wolf-fox as 'about the size of an English hound, but slender with long legs'.

 He wrote:

> It has always been supposed that they are dangerous from the fearless manner in which
> they will venture to approach any person, but I am informed by many well acquainted
> by their habits, that they will do this more from ignorance of the power of man, and
> strong curiosity, than from ferocity, and that they may be easily driven away. They will
> take a piece of meat from the hand, but this habit led to the animal's eventual downfall,
> for with meat in one hand and knife in the other the gauchos killed many of them.

Darwin named the creature *Canis antarcticus*, later to be called *Dusicyon antarcticus australis*. Of this animal he wrote:

> The only quadruped native to the island is a large wolf-like fox (*Canis antarcticus*)
> which is common to both East and West Falkland. I have no doubt it is a peculiar
> species, and confined to this archipelago; because many sealers, Gauchos, and Indians,
> who have visited these islands, all maintain that no such animal is found in any part of
> South America. Molina, from a similarity in habits, thought that this was the same with
> his "culpeu"; (the "culpeu" is the *Canis Magellanicus* brought home by Capt King from
> the Strait of Magellan. It is common in Chile.) But I have seen both, and they are quite
> distinct. These wolves are well known, from Byron's account of their tameness and
> curiosity, which the sailors, who ran into the water to avoid them, mistook for fierce-
> ness. To this day their manners remain the same. They have been observed to enter a
> tent, and actually pull some meat from beneath the head of a sleeping seaman. The
> Gauchos also have frequently in the evening killed them, by holding out a piece of meat
> in one hand, and in the other a knife ready to stick them. As far as I am aware, there is
> no other instance in any part of the world, of so small a mass of broken land, distant
> from a continent, possessing so large an aboriginal quadruped peculiar to itself. Their
> numbers have rapidly decreased; they are already banished from that half of the island
> which lies to the eastward of the Sound. Within a very few years after these islands shall
> have become regularly settled, in all probability this fox will be classed with the dodo,
> as an animal which has perished from the face of the earth.

From descriptions of the animals on West Falkland and East Falkland islands, there are curiously no records of them being found on the other islands. Animals from these different islands were distinct in both size and colour and in 1914 Oldfield Thomas gave them specific names: *Dusicyon darwini* for that of East Falkland and *Dusicyon antarcticus* for that of West Falkland.

Many questions remain unanswered about this animal, the only quadruped found when man first landed on the islands. If, as it has generally been thought, the creature was indigenous, why were there no smaller, less exotic forms of indigenous land mammals, such as rodents? Few records are available about populations, but those that there are indicate that the Warrah was not common; yet food sources in the form of penguins, other birds and marine mammals were plentiful. In a country with very formidable inland areas composed of rocky terrain, stone runs and high hill ranges offering excellent cover to such creatures, it is also curious that such an animal was so easily exterminated over a comparatively short period of time. If, as I believe, this wolf-like fox was a late introduction to the islands, perhaps as late as the early 1600s, how and where did it originate?

Very closely related to the Falkland fox or wolf is the culpeo or South American fox or jackal (*Dusicyon culpaeolus*) at one time common to the southern regions of Chile and the Magellan Straits. It is well known that these animals, or a similar form, were partially domesticated by the indigenous natives of these southern regions. Used as hunting dogs by the Yaghan Indians, these animals were commonly carried on their canoes. Although our wolf-like fox could have arrived in these islands aboard one of these canoes by itself, it is even more plausible that lone groups of Yaghans with their dogs may have been driven out of the protection of the straits and across to the islands in their canoes. Over a long period this could have occurred more than once, with groups being deposited both on East Falkland and West Falkland islands, thus accounting for the apparent difference in the Warrahs of the two main islands.

Slowly, evidence of the Falkland wolf's origins is being gathered together. For me the most intriguing of this evidence is my own discovery of a flint spear head similar to the ones used by the Yaghan Indians of Tierra del Fuego. Discovered on a remote part of the Falklands, could it be evidence of a landing by these Indians and in turn of the origins of the wolf-like fox?

Twenty-five years ago it was possible to stand on certain coastal vantage points and watch migrating whales pass the islands. Many islanders still retain memories of calm evenings and the sound of blowing whales as they made their way through narrow passages in between the islands, either on their way south to feeding grounds or northwards to summer breeding areas. Parts of the islands still bear witness to the days when whales were common; on maps are names such as Whale Passage, Whale Bay, Whale Point and Harpoon Island. Evidence in the form of bleached whalebone litters some coasts but sadly the larger balleen whales themselves are now a rare sight. Occasionally the rarer forms of whale, beaked and toothed whales, are found stranded. In most years groups of blackfish or pilot whales are sighted about the Falklands: it is not uncommon for fairly large numbers of these animals to strand on the islands' shores. There is evidence to suggest that these strandings may be intentional though why the animals strand themselves and why these strandings often occur in the same places will, I am sure, remain one of the mysteries of nature.

The Lady Elizabeth, *Whalebone Cove, East Falkland*

3 The Offshore Islands: A Haven for Wildlife

Clearing Cape Terrible at the north-western extremity of West Point Island, thousands of black-browed albatross and prions skimmed the surface of the sea over the tide rip at this end of the island. The Slipper (Gibraltar Rock) was now on our port side. More than a rock, this island protrudes from the sea like an enormous wedge lying on its side, the thick end rising as a sheer cliff some 91m (300ft) out of the sea. From the top of the cliff down a 45° slope to the thin end of the wedge the entire surface is covered by a dense growth of tussock grass.

A few days earlier I had stood looking out from Cape Terrible towards Gibraltar Rock and beyond. The tide was running at full bore against a south-west wind causing the surface of the water to boil. Even standing ashore the scene made me feel uneasy as I became conscious of the tremendous force of the tide rip. In parts the volume of water being squeezed through the pass between the two islands was such that the level of the tide rip was above that of the surrounding sea by more than 1m (3ft). At the time I wondered how a small boat would fare if caught in this passage. In the 1820s Capt James Weddell wrote of this passage that 'strangers should be careful to avoid these islands in the night time, or in unsettled weather, as the tide runs so strong and irregular through them as to render a ship almost unmanageable'.

On this occasion we had set out from West Point at first light in order to miss the main force of the tide, but with 45km (30 miles) to go out to the further-most of the Jason Island chain, it was inevitable that at some point we would hit one of these tide rips. From West Point Island a chain of offshore islands is spread out in an irregular pattern to the north-west. Generally termed The Jasons, they are made up of varying sized islands, islets and rocks with equally varying and fascinating names: Steeple Jason, Jason West Cay, The Fridays, Elephant Jason, White Rock, South Fur Island and a number of others.

Like the passage between West Point and Gibraltar Rock many of these seaways are narrow, effectively concentrating the flow of water as it passes through. In other regions reefs and underwater ridges create shallow areas. The combination of this chain of islands, their narrow passages, reefs and under-water ridges is in effect a wall protruding from the main Falkland archipelago and across the general flow of the Falkland Current which runs south to north.

To understand more of this current, one must study its origins further south and one of the oceans' greatest sea currents, the Southern Ocean Current. This follows an easterly course to the southward of the South Indian, South Pacific and South Atlantic oceans. For most of its easterly movement this vast current is unrestricted, but as it moves out of the Pacific and into the South Atlantic, the continent of South America thrusts a barrier into the current from the north, a similar barrier from the south being formed by Antarctica's Graham Land Peninsula. Through this comparatively narrow channel, known as the Drake Passage, the Southern Ocean Current is constricted, producing the most notorious of all sea passages in the southern oceans. After passing through the

Current around the islands

60

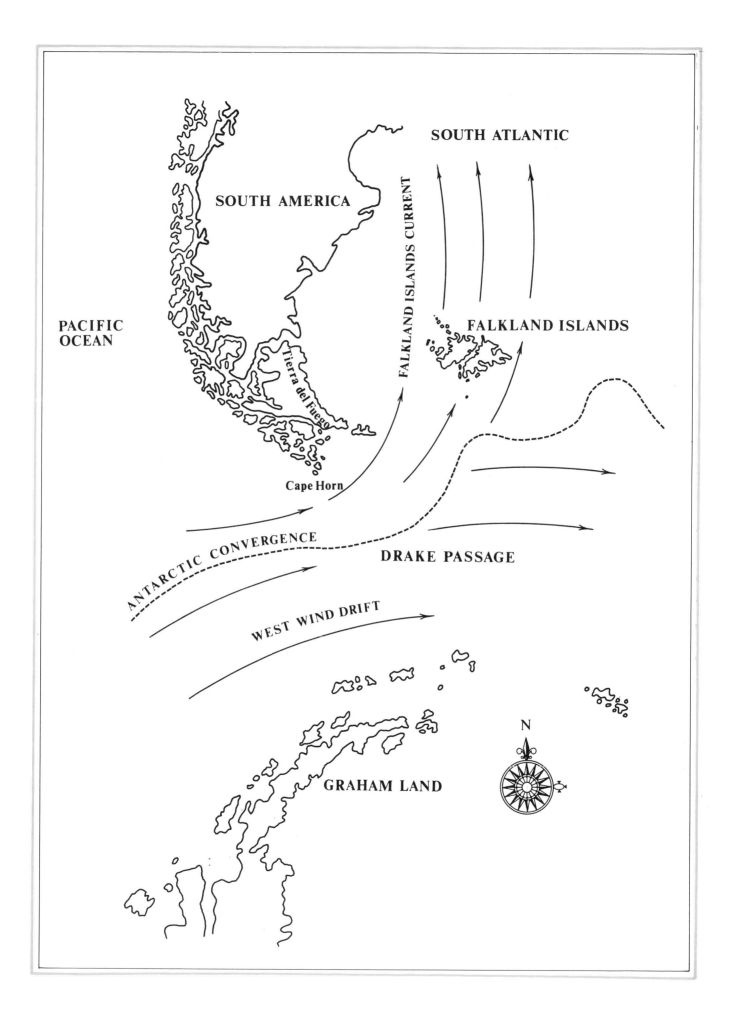

Drake Passage the current spreads, its northern edge curving round the tip of South America.

Parting from the main flow a stream follows a north-easterly direction into the South Atlantic. This, the Falkland Current, then continues its cold stream to approximately latitude 36°S off the southern edge of the Rio de la Plata where it ends. In much the same way that the continent of South America created a barrier to the larger Southern Ocean Current, the Falkland Current's flow is blunted as it meets the archipelago. In effect the main flow is split, one stream flowing round the islands to the south east, the other to the west, resulting in the tide rips I had already seen off West Point Island.

As the current meets the Jason chain it is squeezed between the islands and up and over the reefs and underwater ridges to create the type of tide rip I had observed from Cape Terrible. The complexities of some of these tides are many, depending on the state of the moon, the wind direction and their position in relation to different islands. But in general terms they create a broad sweep of disturbed water from West Point to the outermost islands of Jason East and West Cays, a distance of some 45km (30 miles). On a clear day with the tide running against a wind and with a view of this chain of islands, the broad sweep of tide rips is marked as if a paint brush had drawn a white line over the surface of the sea.

Just as the names of these islands vary, so does their physical appearance. Passing close to South Fur Island, its coastline appeared to be made up of a mass of huge blocks of a dark-coloured rock, the form and shape of which I had not seen anywhere else in the Falklands. Some years later, intrigued by that first view of the island, I was able to make a landing. A close inspection was even more intriguing. Except for a fairly flat central area covered with a deep mat of the coarse spiky grass *Poa robusta* and a most unusual mat formation of tussock grass, a large portion of the island is made up of huge boulders. But they are much larger than I had realised, and far more interesting.

On the more exposed southern side the coastline is built of almost perfectly formed angular shaped blocks, each block measuring upwards of 2.5m (8ft) square, and piled in almost orderly fashion. Behind this orderly formation and strewn inland are smaller boulders, telling a story of a succession of violent seas gradually breaking away the coastal blocks and hurling them inland. The formation of the island made up entirely of these blocks amazed me but the colour I found even more intriguing. All the rock is a dull black with a slight green tinge. Much of the rock lying inland, where most of its weathering is from the action of the wind, is rough and crystalline. When a piece is broken in half crystals can be seen to glitter in the light. On the opposite side of the island where there are gradually shelving beaches the sea has worn the rock debris smooth and to an intense black colour. I had pondered over the general formation of the island, these unusually shaped rocks and their colour, only to realise that the island was formed entirely from an extrusion of an igneous rock. Curiously this is the only site in that chain of islands which shows such a formation.

Already the voyage had shown contrasts between the offshore islands, the wedge shape of Gibraltar Rock, the low boulder formed South Fur Island. Now ahead of us was another island formation, totally different in composition. Rising over 280m (900ft) above sea level, South Jason had been visible on the horizon since leaving West Point. In contrast to most of the islands in this

62

group, South Jason and its sister island Elephant Jason, have their axes running south-west to north-east, almost at right angles to the others and to our own north-westerly course. For some time, therefore, I had been viewing the south-easterly side, a very steep-sloped area with a lush growth of tussock grass from the top of the sharply cut coastal cliffs to the apex of the island. In all a most impressive and formidable piece of terrain, the only flat areas being small plains at both extremities of the island, surrounded by dense coastal belts of tussock grass.

Tussock grass, (*Poa flabellata*), is found growing on most sub-antarctic islands as a maritime formation, thriving best in locations where it is subjected to sea spray and can benefit from the nutrients of seabird and seal colonies. As its common name suggests, the plant forms a tussock and is often referred to in the Falkland Islands as a bog. The plant produces a fibrous pedestal or stool, from the top of which grows a mass of green leaf divided into numerous growing points. The pedestal's centre is formed from the root systems of these growing points. Individual leaves may grow 1–2m (3–6ft) in length from this pedestal, the whole plant often reaching a total height of 2m (6ft) or more.

Approaching an offshore tussock island for the first time I was reminded of some of the descriptions written by the earlier voyagers to the archipelago. They wrote of the coasts and islands being covered by dense woods with trees not unlike palms. Indeed from our position off this island, the tussock grass gave that impression.

Growing as individual plants, the tussock is generally spaced about 30–60cm (1–2ft) apart, forming stands which may cover some smaller islands with an almost impenetrable growth. There are, however, limits to the area of these stands, which appears to be directly controlled by the marine environment in which the plant naturally occurs. Stands rarely extend outside a coastal belt more than 100–200m (150–200yd) in width; at this point vigorous growth declines and other vegetation takes over. It is still not clear what factors ultimately control where the tussock grass will thrive, but it is obvious that it cannot stand competition from other plants. The salt-tolerant nature of *Poa flabellata* and the inability of many other plants to survive a salt-laden maritime environment have an important bearing on its distribution. Additionally, it would appear that tussock benefits nutritionally from sea spray.

One of the most important factors in the growth of tussock grass is the beneficial interaction which exists between the plant and bird and animal life. The latter, utilising tussock islands as breeding and feeding habitats, in turn supply the plant with nutrients and inter-plant cultivation. Birds seeking food in the leaf debris which accumulates between the stools, the burrowing action of petrels and penguins and even the movement of seals between the pedestals, all play an important part in cultivation and prevent competitive plants from becoming established. The tussock receives nutrients directly from guano which is rich in phosphates and nitrogen and is deposited by birds and seals.

It had often puzzled me, though, how tussock grass received its nutrients on some islands where particularly rich stands grew and yet direct methods were not evident. Such sites could hold large colonies of seabirds but these might often be isolated from the stands of grass and in many cases situated at a lower elevation, thus the possibility that nutrients reached the plants by seepage had to be ruled out. One warm day while working on an island which held a large

Giant petrel(Macronectes giganteus) *nesting in tussock fringe*

seabird colony situated several yards below the tussock grass stands, a heavy downpour of rain suddenly turned the colony into a sea of guano-rich mud. Immediately following the downpour, the already warmed surface of the island caused the fallen rain to evaporate. Wisps of vapour rose off the colonies and moved over the tussock stands in the light air. With it came the overpowering stench of guano giving off ammonia fumes and the realisation that this was an indirect but effective way for the grass to receive nitrogen as the vapour condensed on its leaves.

As we reached the southern extremity of South Jason a similar stench came across the water and a large group of fur seal passed our bows, heading for a rocky peninsula off the south end of the island. As is typical of this species when travelling at speed, the animals were porpoising clear of the water, a movement which our other species of seal appear to be incapable of achieving. I knew that a large fur seal colony existed on the rocks off Elephant Jason Island but these animals, unless they suddenly changed direction, appeared to be intent on heading for South Jason. Then I noticed along the top edge of the rocky peninsula the typical staining, dark against the light grey quartzite of the rocks. What I thought at first were eroded tussock grass stools were actually moving; the entire horizon line over the peninsula was alive with fur seal. There had been no previous records of these animals on this island but now it seemed a sizeable colony had established on the point.

Viewing South Jason from its southern point one obtains a completely new perspective and a better impression of its very steep sides. But only when I negotiated the slopes on foot, did I realise how steep the sides are. Even with the tussock grass to hold onto, the south-east side of the island was so steep that a diagonal course had to be taken up the slope. Unlike many tussock grass stands the plants here, although dense and lush, have barely formed stools or pedestals. Instead, the plants tend to throw a mass of green leaf directly out of the soft peaty soil.

Towards the top of the tussock-covered south-east side is a grey quartzite ridge, the main surface of which inclines at the same angle as the tussock slope. Right at the top of the rocky incline the ridge drops off abruptly to the equally steep-sided north-west side. Equally abrupt is the change in the island's environment: on the north-west slope much of the ground is covered with finer grasses only a few inches high with the tussock grass being confined to a narrow coastal belt. The quartzite ridge forming a central backbone to the island is split open in parts and in such places one can walk into a miniature world of calm air and silence.

Breeding group of fur seal (Arctocephalus australis)

On the south-east slope bird life is quite prolific. A colony of black-browed albatross and rockhopper penguins was established about half way up the slope and there were numbers of striated caracara, but on the high ridge the only species I came across was a nesting Paraguayan snipe. In my experience there are no hard and fast rules as to where birds may be found nesting, but I was surprised to find this particular species in what I would have considered to be a hostile environment. As I continued along the ridge another two snipe were seen, so it seems there was a niche at that elevation which suited it.

The south-west end of South Jason forms a long, narrow peninsula, culminating in a rocky point where I had seen the fur seal. This was found to be covered with a very dense stand of tussock grass which gradually gave way further inland to a small plain of fine grasses, most of it composed of mountain blue grass (*Poa alopecurus*) forming small tussocks about 23cm (9in) high. This was some of the most difficult ground to cover as every step had to be placed carefully either to balance on the centre of these grassy tussocks or to find one's boot wedged at an awkward angle between them. But this is nevertheless interesting land for it is an example of how many parts of the Falklands must have been before man introduced sheep and grazed out these fine grasses. In some of the slightly moister areas there were huge patches of the now uncommon sword grass (*Carex trifida*) an attractive sedge with a three-sided stem.

My hope had been to make my way through the tussock grass to the end of the peninsula and so look more closely at the fur seal colony. The grass was often over 2m (6ft) high but, despite its depth and density, I had great hopes of covering the distance of less than 1.5km (1 mile) to the point. I had only gone a short distance when I suddenly came across a large hole. Twenty-five years earlier the island had caught fire and much of the tussock grass was burnt. Records of the damage which was actually done to the island are not precise, although it is recorded that at West Point, watchers at night could see balls of fire careering down the steep south-east side of the island. These were almost certainly burning tussock bogs which had become detached. I knew that in some parts the fire had gone underground, forming huge pits of ash in which one might easily drown.

Capt Charles Barnard, an American sealer who worked about the islands in the early 1800s describes his experiences of such pits:

> We found, from the state of the ground, that the tushooks [tussocks] which grew at some former period, had been burnt, and that the fire had penetrated the earth, in some places, to the depth of thirty or forty feet: the openings of the pits were from six to eight feet square, and greatly widened underground. In many of these pits we saw hair seals and sea lions, which had accidentally fallen in, some of which were dead and others dying . . . we could not get down to them. We were obliged to walk here with great caution, for the tushook grass had grown round those holes so thickly that they could not be perceived until the grass was pulled away.

Being aware of this danger I had continually looked for signs of the fire damage, especially on the south-eastern slopes of the island but had seen nothing. The hole now in front of me dropped directly down perhaps 3m (10ft) and a similar distance across. Changing direction to go round it I suddenly came across another, but this was only 30–60cm (1–2ft) wide, almost covered by tussock leaf. The hole itself was dark and of an unknown depth. Standing on a large tussock pedestal I surveyed my intended route: the peninsula was dotted with tell-tale breaks in the tussock or slight differences in the level of the

Large mixed colony of black-browed albatross, rockhopper penguins and king cormorants nesting on coastal perimeter of offshore tussock island

grass which I decided marked those areas where the fire had gone underground. Keen as I was to reach the fur seal colony, I decided that the risk of falling in or breaking through a surface-covered pit was too high and I turned back.

Later I was presented with the same problem on Elephant Jason Island. This island had also suffered from fire in the spring month of November 1949, caused it is believed by a lightning strike. In this case the island burnt for two years and untold damage must have been caused to the vegetation and the wildlife. On South Jason the charred bases of some tussock pedestals were clear evidence of fire; on Elephant Jason I was surprised to find that many of the tussock stools still bore evidence of fire. Even after so many years the bases remained charred where the normal skirt of dead leaf had been burnt off. I concluded that the fire must have swept through the tussock quickly rather than burnt deeply into the ground. Further evidence of this was the discovery of numerous petrel burrows scorched and black, often with the burnt remains of incubating birds.

Except for a brief period of stocking, Elephant Jason is another example of the few larger islands to survive the often careless introduction of cattle and sheep. The coastal belt of tussock grass, even after the damage sustained as a result of fire, is one of the best examples I have seen. On the south-east slopes of the island, inland and behind the coastal belt of tussock I saw some impressive specimens of *Blechnum* fern. Many plants were over 1m (3ft) high with huge trunks, standing like miniature forests of New Zealand tree ferns. Equally impressive were the enormous cushion-forming balsam plants (*Bolax gummifera*). Measuring up to 4.2m (14ft) in diameter and over 1.2m (4ft) high, such giant growths were probably in existence when man first landed on the islands.

I had often wondered about the name Elephant Jason. Elephant seal could be found on the island's beaches, but hardly in numbers to warrant the island being named after them. The general shape of the island on a modern map bears a crude resemblance to an elephant with its outstretched trunk, this latter feature being represented by a narrow peninsula at the south-west end. But when the island obtained its name maps were neither accurate nor detailed enough to show this resemblance. The answer came as we sailed by the south-west tip of the island and were presented with a view of its north-west slopes. Just below the highest point, an elevation of nearly 213m (700ft), the land fell away sharply to the coastline and then dropped abruptly into the sea. When viewed in profile this part of the island looked like an elephant's leg and foot. Viewed from a north-westerly aspect there were four legs and feet.

I had expected that we would hit the full force of a tide rip at some stage of the journey. This came in the area of water between Elephant Jason and Grand Jason. As the schooner lurched and rolled, Weddell's words came back to me yet again. In normal sea conditions we would expect to be able to make adjustments in the steering to help counter a sea; in this case it appeared hopeless. One minute there would be a respite and the boat would seem to be making headway in comparatively smooth waters, the next instant we were pounded by green waters coming over the boat from all directions.

While travelling through the chain of islands, I had seen bird life very much in evidence but spread out over large areas. Now there were concentrations of birds. Black-browed albatross cruised over the wave tops occasionally alighting on the broken waters, lunging for food and laboriously lifting off again. There

Elephant seal with rockhopper penguins

were terns, silver-grey fulmars, some of the smaller species of storm petrel and large numbers of prions, all intent on feeding on the marine life which was being deposited on the surface by upwelling. This is a funnelling effect caused by currents meeting underwater ridges or being squeezed between reefs and islands and tends to concentrate marine life into the surface layers of the sea.

Now and again the sea around the boat would take on a pinkish colouration as we passed through swarms of krill, or whale feed as it is sometimes known. These are collective names given to different forms of crustacea, the most common form found around the Falkland Islands being a species known as *Munida gregaria* or lobster krill. Occasionally a tern would be seen flying by with one of these creatures in its bill, and many of the other species were doubtless taking this form of feed too. *Munida* also forms an important part of the fur seal's diet and at certain times of the year their colonies are often stained a reddy brown from a carotenoid pigment found in the excreta of seal feeding on this form of krill.

Although krill must swim for survival, since resting means it will sink, the ocean currents are largely responsible for its initial distribution into the regions where I now observed it being swept up onto the surface by the tide rips. Krill

71

Black-browed albatross with chick

King cormorants at nest site

has a natural habit of congregating in very large, dense shoals or swarms, such swarms being commonly recorded 30–60m (100–200ft) in diameter. In areas such as the Jason Island chain, where main movements of water like the Falkland Current are concentrated and restricted, the appearance is that the same may occur to swarms of krill and other forms of marine life, judging by the even larger concentrations observed.

In 1684 William Dampier, a privateer approaching the same islands, had a similar experience and he recorded:

> The day that we made these islands (January 28) we saw great shoals of small lobsters, which coloured the sea in red spots, for a mile in compass, and we drew some out of the sea in our water buckets. They were no bigger than the top of a man's little finger, yet all their claws, both great and small like a lobster.

On one occasion, standing on a high peak overlooking part of the chain of islands, I had noted what at first looked like a layer of sea mist over an island some miles out. A stream of albatross were moving back and forth from the area and it was then I realised that the surface mist was in fact a mass of birds alighted on the sea, feeding on these concentrations of krill or food fields. In this case the field, some 90–180m (100–200yd) in width, stretched for 3km (2 miles) or more and was covered by feeding birds.

One afternoon on New Island, some 60km (40 miles) south of the Jason chain, I had spotted what I thought was a low cloud spread out along the horizon. This, too, turned out to be a mass of birds flying just above the sea. Such were the numbers that they covered the horizon all the way from Grey Channel, an entrance to the south of my vantage point and lying between New Island and Beaver Island, to the east of my position and then out of sight round the northern part of New Island, a distance of some 7.5–9km (5–6 miles). The number of birds in view was staggering; then I realised that the birds were moving in one direction only, with streams of birds coming in from the open sea through Grey Channel. I watched this scene for three or four hours and probably saw hundreds of thousands of birds. They were thin-billed prions, a very common species of petrel nesting in large numbers on New Island and neighbouring islands. Normally they are widely dispersed far out at sea during the day, only appearing over the island at night to return to their nest burrows. The reason for their return to the island in such vast formations and in daylight is not known but it is another illustration of just how vast the bird populations are in these islands, what food resources are available and the importance of these offshore islands as breeding grounds.

Towards the outermost point of the Jason chain lie two of the largest islands, Grand and Steeple Jason. Although lying close together, these two islands show some interesting differences in their formation. Steeple Jason, or St Paul's Island as it was once known, has central ridges running down its longitudinal axis with a maximum elevation of over 274m (900ft). In parts these ridges rise acutely, forming sharply pointed peaks so narrow that it is almost possible to straddle them and look down both sides of the mountain at the same time.

Grand Jason, the larger of the two islands, with a maximum elevation of over 300m (1,000ft), is also topped with an exposed quartzite ridge. In parts this ridge rises sheer-sided but, instead of continuing to form sharply pointed peaks as on Steeple Jason, the ridge tops are broken, presenting a series of flat topped tower-like formations. Immediately below this ridge, huge boulders and other

74

rock debris lies scattered on the southern slopes of the island, forming miniature stone runs which terminate on the coast. In contrast, the slopes below the ridges on Steeple Jason are clear of rock debris, giving the impression that a breaking down of its peaks has yet to commence.

Although remote and lying 45km (30 miles) from the mainland of West Falkland, both islands have a history of farming going back to the late 1870s. Before that there are records of sealing and penguin oiling, the latter on a very extensive scale. The penguin oiling industry has fascinated me ever since I found trypots on the coast of Grand Jason. On Steeple Jason there are the remains of many try works along the south coast and although the pots used for boiling down the penguins have gone, piles of burnt bones, stone corrals and the oilers' small stone shelters all remain, showing the extent of the penguin oiling industry. Rockhopper penguins appeared to have suffered most, as the corrals were centred on existing rockhopper penguin rookeries and the charred bones piled 60–80cm (2–3ft) high are of this species. Records confirm that the rockhopper was the species most used by the oilers, but I have never seen mention of gentoo penguins being taken. However, it is unlikely that the oilers would have been careful to avoid gentoos and, before I left Steeple Jason, I made a discovery that showed that this species, too, had suffered.

The peaks of Steeple Jason Island

75

Making my way to the west end of the island one morning, I decided to walk along the northern slopes of the backbone of hills so that I could look down over the wide plain that stretched along the north coast. Above the gentoo grounds a low col breaks through the hills, giving an easy route to the south. Coming abreast of this col and looking down towards the gentoos, I saw two parallel lines of rocks running diagonally in the direction of the gentoo colony. These lines were spaced about 3m (10ft) apart and stretched for over 457m (500yd); they were clearly man-made and ran from the colony to the col.

After visiting the site several times I concluded that these lines of stones must have been retaining walls and that they had perhaps marked a route by which rockhopper penguins had been driven over from the south side of the island to try works in the north. Where the gentoo penguins came ashore there was a deep gulch that would have made an ideal landing and loading spot for casks of oil, so it seemed that the oilers had decided that it was better to drive the birds closer to where the oil could be loaded. However, though I thoroughly inspected the area by the gentoo colony, I could not find signs of a try works. The nearest try works, and substantial ones at that, were on the south side of the col. This eventually led me to wonder whether the movement could have been the other way round with the gentoo penguins being driven to try works on the south.

The more thought I gave to this idea, the more certain I became that it was right. The gentoo is quicker and more nervous than the rockhopper and the oilers might well have taken advantage of its natural instinct to move inland when breeding. When the birds had been rendered down, the full casks of oil could have been rolled down the gentle slope to the north shore, perhaps using the same walled route. This would then have served a double purpose and all the rendering down would have been done on the south side of the island.

I have not been able to date the workings near the south side of the col. Although I found records about oiling on Steeple and Grand Jason Islands, I feel sure that these works are older than those actually recorded. It is clear, however, that many thousands of penguins were killed for their oil. The recorded industry reached a peak in about 1864, and between 1863 and 1866 a total of 286,000 litres (63,000 gal) of oil were shipped to Stanley. Records indicate that the oilers expected to obtain 4.5 litres (1 gal) of oil from eight rockhopper penguins, so in those three years alone over half a million penguins were killed and rendered down.

In the latter half of the 1700s and early 1800s American whaling and sealing expeditions used the Falkland Islands as a shore-base for their operations about the islands and as a staging post for voyages farther south and round Cape Horn into the Pacific. The exact date when the Falklands were first visited by these whaling expeditions is not clear, for these exploiters were often secretive about their hunting grounds, but writings about the whalers from Nantucket dated 1771 indicate that the Falklands had been visited by these men before this time. There is also a record of an expedition of several vessels having made a voyage in 1775.

One of the earlier documented voyages to the Falklands was by a ship called the *States*. Owned by William Rotch, a Quaker whale oil merchant from Nantucket, the *States*, under Capt Benjamin Hussey, sailed for the islands in late 1784, by which time it was no secret that seals were numerous about the archipelago. With the *States* was the whaleship *Mary*, under Capt Shubael

Rockhopper penguins coming ashore on a formidable coastline

76

New Island, Beaver Island, from the Weddell Island group

Coffin. In the history of the New England whalemen, Nantucket Island, its little colony of mainly Quaker whalemen and the names of Rotch and Coffin are famous. The same names were to become linked with the Falklands and today remain as an intriguing reminder of the islands' past history and its close connection with the whalers from the north-eastern seaboard of the USA over two hundred years ago. It is not clear where the first expeditions of whalers to the Falklands made landfall but there is little doubt that the small archipelago in the south-west corner of the Falkland group was very quickly to become their self-styled home.

New Island, with its excellent harbours, may have been the first such home, being named perhaps as early as 1775 after New England's seaports such as New London, New York, New Haven and New Bedford. It may even have been a member of the Coffin family who first sailed into and named New Island, for the island once had a Coffin Harbour and has today, protecting its entrance, Coffin Island.

Beaver Island was almost certainly named after one of two famous whaleships called *Beaver*; either the vessel which featured in the 1773 Boston tea party incident, or a later vessel which bears the distinction of having been the first American whaleship to double Cape Horn in 1791. Between Beaver Island

and Weddell Island, known by the early whalers as Swan Island, lie some twenty smaller islands, many of them bearing names linked to the Quakers of Nantucket and their whalers: Penn Island, Barclay Island, both Rotch vessels named after whalemen; Governor Island, Little Coffin Island, Quaker Island and Quaker Harbour. Others are Pitt Island and States Harbour, the latter doubtless named after the vessel *States* and her voyage of 1784.

Sadly many of these islands also bear the scars of these past exploiters. Not only did the islands offer excellent shelter for their ships, from where they could launch whaling and sealing operations, but smaller accessible islands with their cover of tussock grass were ideal sites for holding fresh meat supplies in the form of pigs, goats and rabbits. In his narrative dated 1812–16 Capt Barnard gives a clear and interesting account of this practice and of how these islands suffered in other ways.

Barnard then goes on to relate his discovery of some pigs on Weddell Island:

While rowing along the shore of this island we discovered a number of hogs near the beach, and landed undiscovered by them; the dog caught a large sow big with pig, and a young boar; we tied their legs, and took them alive with us to New Island, and turned them loose on the south end. We thought it would be to our benefit to bring over a number alive, and establish the breed on the south as well as on the north end of the island, where they bred and throve well.

Of a pig hunt on New Island Barnard wrote:

> . . . our pork being expended and the weather too stormy to go to Beaver Island after more, we made search on this island [New Island], being confident that there were one or two young litters from a boar and two sows which we had left here on our first arrival, which was more than twelve months since. They had kept themselves so concealed among the high tushooks, in a remote part of the island, that we seldom saw any signs of them: however, on hunting with the dog, he soon took the scent, and pulled hard to get from the man who held the string, as if desirous of going in a different direction from ours. We followed him more than a mile without seeing any hogs, when entering the tushooks on a sudden, he was loose, and in a few minutes we heard a pig squeal; and we knew by the weak sound that it was a small one. When the dog finds a boar in the tushooks, we are obliged to approach the spot with great caution, and call the dog away; but now we approached it without fear and found that he had captured a fine fat pig.

The introduction of pigs, goats and, in a few cases, rabbits was to cause considerable damage to the islands' vegetation, but the habit of firing tussock grass, also described by Barnard, was to cause more serious and lasting damage:

> On the 14th December, I discovered a smoke rising from Beaver Island, which I knew was occasioned by some persons setting fire to the tushooks, that being the method here of making signals of distress, or when various parties are sealing on different islands, and wish to communicate, or convey information to one another. For instance, two gangs may be out sealing, only one of which has a boat; when the one has procured all the skins, they wish the boat or shallop to come and take them and their fare off; for a signal to that effect they set fire to the tushooks . . . If fire is kindled there, it will continue burning several days; and when it communicates to the bogs, or penetrates below the surface of the soil, which it most commonly does, it will burn several months, and make deep chasms or pits in the ground.

Few of the islands in the south west of the archipelago now hold stands of tussock grass, many bearing signs of past burning, evident by layers of deep red ash often some feet below the present layers of soil. In extreme cases erosion set in after burning and gradually, over the years, wind and rain have reduced many areas to a landscape of clay and rock. On a number of these islands, the native boxwood (*Hebe elliptica*) still survives, although I suspect fire also played a part in destroying what must have been more extensive areas of this evergreen shrub. Growing to a height of 3.6m (12ft), boxwood, which is restricted to West Falkland, is today more commonly found growing as scattered bushes on rocky coastal edges, although a few dense stands covering several acres survive on some islands.

Like the Jason Island chain, the south-westerly group has an impressive scenic beauty but contrasts greatly with the former region. Much of the west and south-west coast rises abruptly out of the sea, forming sheer-sided cliffs which on parts of Beaver Island and New Island, are over 152m (500ft) high. Centuries of continuous pounding of their weather side shores by heavy seas have carved out the softer layers of rock to create cliffs of breathtaking form and dimensions. In many parts the cliffs are undercut, giving the impression that some invisible hand is all that holds the coast from toppling into the sea. Sea caves of unknown depth continually swallow and spew out foaming seas which never seem still.

Looking south from New Island across Grey Channel to Beaver and Weddell Islands one may be taken back in time to the days of sail for, apparently making a course out of Beaver Island and heading for the mouth of Grey Channel, are two vessels under sail. Known as The Colliers, these sea stacks, cut by wind

The Horse Block Stack, West Falkland

Inset: Landsend Bluff, New Island

80

Black oystercatcher (Haematopus ater)

Adult pair of flightless steamer duck (Tachyeres brachypterus), *a common species of marine duck*

The western cliffs of New Island

and sea, are typical of the region. Off the south-west coast of Weddell Island the Horse Block stack rises like the Trojan horse, so convincing is it in shape that it might have been built specially by some ancient cult.

Where the coasts have fallen away or the action of sea and wind has cut through high cliffs, free-standing bluffs or stacks have been formed. Sheer-sided and rising hundreds of feet, there is something both formidable and magical about them.

Although New Island, Beaver Island and the Weddell group of islands offered the early whalers excellent anchorages and shore bases, there were other attractions to the region. It is recorded that in the bays of New Island whales would come to calf. There were also known whale passages between the islands, and it became a practice of the whalemen to post lookouts on the high points of islands like New Island to signal to their tenders in the harbours below when whales were sighted approaching.

During the years between 1785 and 1810 there developed in New England what was to be known as the whaleman-sealer. Francis Rotch was probably the first American merchant to recognise the importance of the sealing industry. A letter to one of his whaling masters who was to over-winter at the Falklands stated that if the prospects were there, to advance the voyage during the winter, he should engage in the 'seal fisherie and other ways' and that 'you will not think of rejecting such an opportunity'. The 'seal fishery', unspecific in its terminology, was intent on two commodities: oil from the elephant seal and skins from the fur seal, although probably inexperienced crews took sea lions also.

View from Staats Island to south west coast of Weddell Island

Staats Island Bluff, West Falkland

Cliffs cut by the action of seas form stacks of amazing shape

Fur seal on New Island

View from West Point Island across the 'Woolly Gut' to Death's Head, West Falkland

Fur seals were common on the formidable west and south-west coasts of New Island, Beaver Island and Staats Island and, although they are not in such large numbers as in earlier times, this region is still an important breeding ground.

Capt Barnard gives an account of one of the New Island fur seal colonies and of the lengths to which these men went to secure skins:

On the 25th we went down a steep gully, formed by a wide rent in the rocks, extending from the tops of the cliffs, and leading through to the sea, in quest of fur seals and their pups; we descended to the sea, and clambered along the rocks towards the place where we had seen the seals in great abundance; but though we were near to them, we were prevented from going any further by the sea rolling under the cliffs, the bases of which, by the continual action of the sea, had been hollowed out and formed into deep caverns. To effect a passage over this place, Louder, who was a good swimmer, took one end of a rope, and swam with it to the other side, where he was followed by Green. We on this side fastened Ansel, who could not swim, to the middle of the rope, and lowered him away, while those on the other side hauled him over, without his even touching the water, which was very cold. I then swam across, leaving Albrook to send our knives, steels, clubs, and clothes across, by securing them to the middle of the line, which we drew over. There we found a large number of seals, which were very tame, and easy to kill; probably they had never been visited or disturbed by man, in this almost inaccessible retreat. We took about one hundred and twenty, mostly pups, and remained all night, which we passed most uncomfortably on the rocks, in this cold and exposed situation.

We finished skinning the seals, and carried them to the hauling place, and by means of the rope and the man on the other side, got them safely across this dangerous current. We waited for a smooth time before we crossed, and then two of us plunged into the water, among a great many seals, who were playing and jumping about in the briny flood. The one who remained with Ansel, lowered him, while we hauled him over. After all were across, we carried the skins to the foot of the ravine, and left them there: we ascended to the top, and then proceeded to our residence, distant about one mile. We immediately prepared something to eat, and then retired to rest; both of which we absolutely needed.

We went for the skins on the following morning. When we arrived at the cliffs, we attached one end of the rope to a stake, and carried the other down with us as far as it would reach, to assist us in regaining the top with our burdens; which consisted of five or six skins for each. Having in this laborious manner conveyed all the skins to the top the severest part of the labour was yet to be completed. After a short intermission we resumed our task, and carried the skins to the place denominated our home, and placed them all in a pile. I then directed that all should stand round it, and that each man should draw a skin in rotation, and put it to what use he thought proper, which would prevent all disputes in washing and drying them. This mode of distribution I established as a general rule, and it was cheerfully agreed to by the others.

Another interesting narrative from an account written in 1796 by a member of the vessel *Neptune* of New Haven also gives a brief insight into the operation:

. . . Ashore with others to take care of the seal skins, and it being very late in the day, the first thing I thought of was where to take up sleep that night. Searching, I found a few logs which I concluded to make me a little house; though in my search I found a few whale bones which was of great service in building the ruff of my little house . . . Went to Fox Point for sea-elephant oil . . . no food except mussels and maidenweed steeped to drink. Captain Greene arrived in the shallop, bringing food and four thousand more skins to cure. Some geese were shot for a luxurious repast, and several wild hogs were cornered and shot. Forbes reported killing "two loggerhead ducks which weighed 20 lbs each".

In the Falkland Islands today there may be some twenty thousand fur seal spread over about eight main breeding sites. What numbers there were at the time men like Barnard were working the islands is far from clear. These men had little interest in statistics and were secretive about where they obtained skins. There is also some question about the type of seal being taken and almost certainly many sealers took sea lion skins in mistake for fur seal. The records that do exist, however, show that the fur seal was far more common and found at many more sites than it is today. From Barnard's narrative above it is known that fur seal were to be found on islands such as Tea Island and Sea Dog Island. The latter name suggests this island was an important site and this is confirmed by Barnard:

> We now concluded to go to Sea Dog Island for fur seal skins, on which there is but a small landing which is very difficult even in fair weather . . . We discovered that the two men on Sea Dog Island had set fire to the small bundle of tushooks on the top of the rock. This was the signal they had obtained all the skins in their power. We launched the boat and brought them back with the skins, being about eighty large and small.

When Barnard recorded this episode it was February, a time when the seal would still be tending pups, hence his mention of 'large and small'; it is not surprising, therefore, that this island is one of many where fur seal are no longer found.

In the same locality as Sea Dog Island lies Bird Island, a small but rugged island largely covered with dense tussock grass. Like so many offshore islands, Bird Island has a character of its own. More than two thirds of its area forms a wedge shape, much of the northern shore forming the thinner end and being made up of inclined rock faces; the southerly aspects rise to form sheer cut cliffs with elevations of 60m (200ft). Slicing into the wedge, both from the northern and southern shores, deep fissures almost divide the island into separate sections. In many parts these fissures are so narrow that the tussock grass effectively hides them, the only warning of their position being the low murmur of the sea or occasional bark from fur seal far below.

In complete contrast to the wedge shaped section of the island and almost as though a different island had been thrust onto its southern shores is a promontory making up the remaining third of Bird Island's total area. Its main axis lies roughly south to north and therefore protrudes at right angles to the wedge. Much of its coastline is sheer cliff face, but the top surface of the island, unlike the generally flat inclined surface of the wedge, is composed of dome-shaped hills with here and there huge, upstanding rocky stacks which are pitted and eroded away into most unususal shapes. Rock debris is strewn over some of these domed hills, the impression being that at one time the hills were composed of sharp peaks which have been gradually broken away.

Amongst the rocky debris and on the medium and lower slopes of these hills are compact colonies of black-browed albatross and rockhopper penguins. Elsewhere on the hills dense tussock grass forms a habitat for large populations of that beautiful form of petrel, the thin-billed prion. So dense are some of these populations that their burrowing into the ground beneath the tussock stools has caused changes in the plants' growth. Instead of individual stools or tussocks forming, a mass of leaf grows like a mat from a base of deep, loose soil continually cultivated by the burrowing of so many birds.

On my first visit to Bird Island, in 1968, I found only a handful of fur seal but evidence suggested that at one time the island had been an important breeding ground. On one of the island's very few landing places I discovered the remains of an old sealing trypot; one side was broken but I was able to calculate that the pot had been approximately 1.2m (4ft) in diameter and about 60cm (2ft) deep.

South Fur Island, its coastline made up of huge blocks of dark coloured rock

Vegetation on the higher elevations of an offshore island

Breeding group of elephant seals on a typical north coast beach, East Falkland

West coast cliffs of New Island

Tea Island Bluff and south west coast of Weddell Island

Some distance away were signs of habitation: an old ship's timber, a piece of lead and, protruding from the peat, a square metal shaft which when fully unearthed turned out to be a sealing lance. In the same area I uncovered a handmade leather sandal and, perhaps most exciting of all, an old handblown glass bottle of a lovely green-brown shade.

The peaty ground where I had made these discoveries had once been covered by large tussock stools but was now worn away by the passage of seals. I could only conclude that my visit had been very timely, coinciding with a point when the artifacts preserved by layers of peat had been uncovered by the movement of seals but before they had become too exposed and destroyed. The trypot and lance may well have been used for sea lion, but I suspected the main quarry had been fur seal.

Although on this particular visit I only saw some thirty of these animals, the coasts had a fur seal look and feel about them. Having looked at many sites used by this particular seal I believed it no coincidence that such places had similar characteristics. Deep water immediately off breeding sites is one feature and the sites themselves are all on slightly inclined rock faces, often on coasts of deeply stratified cliffs where the animals can climb to fairly high elevations. Shade also appears to be important, especially on breeding sites where young pups can crawl between rock slabs or into deep shady fissures. Over centuries of use, such sites become worn by movement; even the hardest of quartzite becomes polished and in some cases I have come across slabs of rock scored and polished by the nails and flippers of climbing seal.

On Bird Island I found several sites where coastal rocks were highly polished and which presented that look and feel of one-time fur seal haunts, but I never saw the animals themselves in any quantity. It has taken over twenty years of waiting and occasional checking but now, at last, the animals are back. There are only a few, but are precisely where I believe men like Barnard had once taken these seal.

Much of the West Falkland and the offshore islands already described are predominantly composed of Palaeozoic sedimentary rocks, quartzites, sandstones and shales. In the region of Bird Island, on the West Falkland mainland coast and, to a lesser degree, at sites west of Weddell Island, at New Island and South Fur Island, there are also outcrops of metamorphic and igneous rocks of the Archaean basement complex. Folding was the major structural influence in the islands. These folds, composed of Devona-carboniferous rocks of the Palaeozoic era, give rise to the mountain ranges which cross the northern regions of both East and West Falkland. These in turn have influenced the physical appearance and composition of the more spectacular islands adjacent to the north-west, west and south-west of West Falkland.

In sharp contrast to these more spectacular regions, the islands located in the Falkland Sound and to the south and south east of the Lafonia region of East Falkland and this area itself, are generally flat and low lying. Composed of the younger Mesozoic rocks, sandstones and mudstones laid down in the Triassic and Jurassic ages, these Lafonian rocks are disturbed little by any form of folding. This great plain has an average height above sea level of some 15m (50ft) and seldom rises to more than 30m (100ft). With one or two exceptions, the islands in these particular regions show the influence of man's settlement and stocking more than any other area of the Falkland archipelago.

Drafting sheep, Carcass Island

Rockhopper penguins preening and drying off

Robert Cunningham, naturalist aboard HMS *Nassau* which made a voyage to the Falkland Islands and the Straits of Magellan in the years 1866–9, wrote of these islands:

We entered the Sound in the course of the afternoon, and were agreeably surprised by finding the scenery on either side of a considerably more attractive character than in the neighbourhood of Stanley – the land presenting a less barren appearance, and the groves of tussac-grass, which here we saw for the first time in luxuriance, imparting a pleasing shade of green to the landscape, the quiet evening light also contributing to "lend enchantment to the view" . . . Next morning we moved on to the Tyssen Islands, only a few miles from our last night's position . . . Early in the forenoon a number of us landed on the largest island of the group . . . This island was, I should think, about a mile or a mile and a half long, and was girdled with a broad belt of tussac . . . This was the first opportunity that I enjoyed of visiting a tussac grove, and it made a most striking impression on my mind as I wended my way along the narrow winding natural pathways between the separate clumps of grass, the leaves of which waved high overhead in graceful curves. The average height of the plants I should estimate as between ten and twelve feet, while the mass of roots belonging to each varied from a foot to a foot and a half in height by two to three feet in diameter. Among the roots jackass penguins had formed their burrows in numbers, and as we walked through the groves we were accompanied by numerous individuals of a little dusky-brown bird, which, when we sat down, came quite close to us, being even more familiar than our English robin, a specimen on one occasion lighting on one of the sportsmen who was lying in wait for geese, and hopping over him in the most unconcerned manner. The military starling was also common, and hardly less tame.

After a time I ascended to the summit of the island through a gap in the tussac, meeting with specimens of a very stout tall-growing *Carex*, and several Compositae, and finding the Falkland Island tea-plant, *Myrtus nummularia*, and *Rubus geoides*, covering the surface of the ground for yards, the beautiful red fruits of the latter half buried in the moss of the soil.

Accessibility to the main sheep farming region of East Falkland, comparative ease of landing and working on islands with lower elevations, all had its influence on the use of these islands. Over a period of time stocking by both sheep and cattle has changed the majority of these islands dramatically and Cunningham's description probably no longer fitted this scene by the early 1900s.

Unfortunately accounts like Cunningham's are few and we are left today with a rather incomplete picture of what the islands were like before the introduction of stock. In a very few areas, some of which have been described, it is still possible to draw some comparisons between islands that have been stocked and those that have had no history of stocking whatsoever. One such comparison, found off the south-east corner of the archipelago, is Sea Lion Island and an adjacent island, Sea Lion Easterly.

Although a considerable size difference exists between the two islands, topographically they are the same and they are close enough to experience the same weather conditions. Sea Lion Island was not stocked until quite late in the history of farming in the Falklands, and then initially with cattle only. This, according to local records, was due to the very soft boggy nature of this island's terrain, the vegetation and conditions being unsuitable for sheep. Today, the ground under the even-surfaced grassland meadows of the island is firm, in parts springy, but dry. There are large areas of diddle-dee (*Empetrum rubrum*) and other plants generally associated with the drier heath and the sheep which now stock the island do well. A fairly high percentage of the island's original coastal belt of tussock grass remains, having been carefully farmed by a succession of owners who appreciated its value. Many of the tussock stands are deep, indicating that in all probability they represent the original tussocks that existed when the island was first stocked. However, changes have occurred even though stock has had restricted access to areas of this grass.

Landing on the neighbouring Sea Lion Easterly I was immediately confronted with an almost impenetrable coastal belt of not only deep, but dense, tussock grass. Passage through the Sea Lion Island tussock could be carried out with relative ease, the majority of the tussock plants standing clear of each other where the grazing of cattle and sheep had cleared growth and leaf debris away. On Sea Lion Easterly the tussock leaf growth entwines to form a canopy. Successive years of leaf debris cling to the tussock stools leaving little space between the plants. Where light penetrates to the floor between the tussocks, wild celery (*Apium australe*) grows in profusion. Within the stands, the generally firm but spongy ground is much damper than that of the Sea Lion Island tussock areas.

The central meadow of the easterly island instantly reminded me of the remarks made to me about Sea Lion Island having once been 'soft and boggy'. While Sea Lion Island itself was now parched and suffering the effect of a long period without rains, I was walking through a deep green meadow, totally different in its range of plants. Here the ground is uneven from the formation of smaller grass bogs between which there grow thick spongy layers of *Ranunculus* species and the normally small, creeping plant *Pratia repens*, which here forms pure mats with leaves larger than a thumbnail. Intersecting large areas of the meadow are small fissures some 10–15cm (4–6in) deep, the bottom of which is composed of thick, peaty mud. Snipe ran about these fissures, the mud being peppered with small round holes where the birds had been probing for food. Native woodrush (*Luzula alopecurus*) is common to both islands, but on Sea Lion Easterly it has the most luxuriant growth, surpassing anything I found on the larger island. Almost pure stands grow with their cotton-like flower forming a field of nodding heads on tall stems. Between the inside perimeter of the coastal tussock stands and the meadow, the now rare sword grass (*Carex trifida*) grows in huge clumps. This species disappeared from Sea Lion Island soon after the introduction of stock.

Looking over Sea Lion Easterly one could clearly see how the neighbouring island had been changed. With the removal of the more lush vegetation by stock, evaporation of water from the island's surface increased. Gradually the water table lowered, causing physical changes to take place in the peaty soils. The movement of stock physically changed the surface of the meadows, compressing and levelling, with the result that changes also took place in the type of climax vegetation. On Sea Lion Easterly I had only found one or two small patches of diddle-dee but I felt sure that, had this island been subjected to the same physical changes as Sea Lion Island, this heath would quickly have become the dominant vegetation.

South-east of Sea Lion Island lies the most remote island of the Falkland archipelago. Beauchene Island, when I first visited it in December 1963, had been left, untouched, for nearly fifty years. As with so many of the more remote islands, it was fur seal which had been the attraction to man. Then, with the almost complete disappearance of these animals and their protection by law in the early 1900s, the fur seal and their breeding sites were left, almost forgotten.

Beauchene Island always had a reputation for fur seal, locally believed to be

the largest breeding site in the Falklands. As far back as 1792 Edmund Fanning referred to fur seal on this island:

> *Fur Seals.* Of these there are three different grades: full aged males, called wigs; the females, clapmatches; those not quite so old, bulls; all the half-grown of both, yearlings; the young of near a year old, called gray or silvered pups, and before their coats are changed to this color, called black pups. This animal is much more sprightly and active on shore than the elephant, leopard, or hair seal; their chief delight is in the heavy surf on a rough or rocky shore; still, by the accompanying plate it will be noticed they can manage to get themselves quite elevated in the world at times. Here, on the top of a rock forming the NE head of Beauchene Island, situated twenty leagues SE of the Falkland Islands, they can be seen as having attained a place of apparently perfect security from the attack of those seamen who have landed from the boat at its foot, as the elevation of this rookery is between two and three hundred feet, the ascent thereto being over a succession of shelving rocks, and black and white cliffs. The fur seals and their pups, it will be observed, literally cover the top of this rock; some can also be seen in the water swimming for the shore, some upon the lowest part of the rock, others again half way up, or resting upon the cliffs. A few feet beyond the tussuck grass was another flat rock, covered in a similar manner with seals.
>
> The taking of the animals at this place was commenced at dawn of day; after overcoming the difficulty in climbing up, the seamen were obliged to be very cautious of their footing, the extreme slipperiness rendering them liable every moment to slide off, or else the set on of some bristling old wig (bull seal) while defending his charge, would surely send them there from, down the precipice to instant death.

It was fur seal which was to draw me, too, to this remote outlyer, but for a very different reason than that which had taken men there years before. I had wondered just how many of these seal were now to be found after being left undisturbed for nearly half a century.

Beauchene Island is not a large island, being just over 3km (2 miles) in length and proportionately narrow, the widest point being 822m (900yd), the main axis of the island lying approximately north to south. The entire coastline is rugged with varying elevations, although the higher, more formidable coast lies on the north-east corner, extends along much of the east side, culminating at the southern end of the island in a fortress-like, sheer-sided rocky promontory to which I was eventually to refer as The Citadel.

Although Sea Lion Island and the south-east corner of East Falkland are the nearest landfall, the geological composition of Beauchene is more in keeping with that of the south and south-west corners of West Falkland. Much of the island is composed of a light greyish quartzite, the higher more exposed southern section of the island being made up of layers of varying thickness, much of the surface and thinner layers forming a mass of broken debris. At the southern end, fissures cut across the main axis of the island almost dividing it into a number of separate stacks. Along the eastern coastal cliffs, several sea caves cut beneath the island, one breaking out in the centre of the island like a large blowhole.

Much of the northern section of the island is composed of a plateau which slopes gently from the sheer cliffs on the east side to boulder beaches and shelving rock on the west and north-west coasts. This plateau, which forms the broadest section of the island and represents more than two thirds of its surface, is covered by dense tussock grass except for a broad strip of rocky strewn ground which sweeps along the west coast.

At the time of my first landing it was mid-summer. Fur seal would have been breeding, but not a single animal could be found. At the location described by

*The 'Citadel',
Beauchene Island*

103

Fanning, that look and feel of a fur seal colony was distinct. Climbing up over 'a succession of shelving rocks' the surface in parts was highly polished, 'the extreme slipperiness rendering one liable every moment to slide off'. But there were no 'bristling old wig' bull seals to lunge at me. On the edge of the shelving rock slabs there were polished score marks where perhaps for thousands of years seal had ascended the rocks. Except for a small group of rockhopper penguins nesting amongst the rock debris on the perimeter of the old seal colony, the slabs were devoid of life. What the fate of this particular colony might have been is not recorded, but it is known that two sealers who had been the last to land on the island in the early 1900s had, after a month's stay there, only secured some half a dozen skins. This, I believe, was the final blow to the Beauchene Island population of seals.

During a search for some shelter I selected some flat rocks at the head of a small cove. Sealers of 150 years ago must have picked the same site, for engraved on the rock slabs were several inscriptions with dates, the earliest being 1834 against the name W. Blinn who, I later discovered, sailed from New Bedford in 1834 for a sealing voyage to the Falklands. I also found the remains of a trypot and, in a cleft between some huge slabs of rock, evidence of a makeshift shelter where sealers would have made a temporary home.

The discovery that the fur seal were no longer on the island had been a great disappointment but this was partly obscured by another find. I had known of the existence of a colony of rockhopper penguins and black-browed albatross on the island but had not been prepared for the number of birds on the coast-line on the west side of the island. The rocky strewn area, from the perimeter of the tussock to the sea, was packed so densely with nesting albatross and penguins that the birds were continually squabbling to hold their territories. The number of birds which made up this colony must have ranged between one and two million – the greatest density of these two species I came across anywhere in the archipelago.

It was on Beauchene Island that I was first introduced to one of the southern hemisphere's rarest birds of prey. The striated caracara (*Phalcoboenus australis*) or Johnny rook as it is known locally, is found only in the Falklands and on a number of remote islets off Cape Horn and Southern Chile.

When I landed on Beauchene several of these birds had appeared, obviously very inquisitive of this intruder. No sooner had I placed my rucksack down on the rocks and moved a little distance away than two or three of these raptors were picking and pulling at the flaps!

Nineteenth century accounts of the Falkland Islands refer to this bold and inquisitive raptor, a caracara or carrion eater. Early mariners labelled the raven-sized birds sea eagles or rooks, then later Johnny rooks. I had puzzled over the name until I landed on a remote island in the Falkland archipelago; like Beauchene, one of the few remaining strongholds of the species. There I saw a sight that must have presented itself to the sealers and penguin oilers who had walked these shores more than 150 years earlier: on a coastal green, large groups of gentoo penguins were busy building nests. Stationed around the colony's perimeters were the dark, silent 'rooks', watching and waiting. I had seen a similar scene in England: rooks on freshly turned pasture. I remembered, too, that to the nineteenth century whalers and sealers, the gentoo penguin was known as Johnny penguin; here, surely, was the derivation of the name Johnny rook.

Striated caracara (Phalcoboenus australis)

105

Charles Barnard described the bird and discussed its early naming:

These birds, generally known among sealers by the name of rooks, partake of the form and nature both of the hawk and the crow. They are about the size of the largest hen hawks common to the United States; of a black color, and shaped something like a rook. Their claws are armed with large and strong talons, like those of an eagle; they are exceedingly bold and the most mischievous of all the feathered creation. The sailors who visit these islands, being often much vexed at their predatory tricks, have bestowed different names on them, characteristic of their nature, as flying monkeys, flying devils, etc etc. I have known these birds to fly away with caps, mittens, stockings, powder horns, knives, steels, tin pots, in fact every thing which their great strength is equal to. On landing at any place, we always find some of these birds, who visit us for the purpose of reconnoitering; and if we have any meat in the boat, they give the signal by commencing such an ear-tormenting cawing, that we are soon surrounded by additional numbers; they compel us to secure our provisions, by covering them with the sails of the boat, which we fastened down by stones, and then direct the dog to lie down by them to prevent these harpies from hauling off the stones and sails, to get at and devour the provisions. These winged pirates have been known to attack a man, when passing near their nests while their young ones were there. From their color, mischievous disposition, and feeding on carrion, they appear to belong to the crow species; while, on the other hand, from the size (being twice that of the common crow), strength, audacious boldness, their form, and largeness of their talons, they appear to be connected with the hawk, which, when pinched with hunger, have been known to feed on carrion. I should, from these characteristics, call them the vulture-crow. I shall, however, continue to distinguish them by the name they are most generally called by sealers, viz. rooks, until some ornithologist shall affix to them their appropriate name.

When Charles Darwin visited the islands he found this species to be 'exceedingly common'. Darwin's two short visits to the Falklands – in March of 1833 and 1834 – were to the north of the main island of East Falkland and in particular to Port Louis, at that time the only settlement in the islands. Today the species is rarely seen in this region of the archipelago and then only as a vagrant. Yet Johnny ROOKS are common in their few remaining breeding areas, especially in the west part of the Falklands. Like Barnard, Darwin and other naturalists have written of the species' scavenging, carrion-eating habits; the result is a picture of a tenacious, survivor species.

Why, given its adaptability, did the striated caracara disappear from its former stronghold in East Falkland and in the other main islands? When Darwin visited the islands less than a hundred settlers lived in the Falklands, and sheep farming, the islands' chief occupation today, had yet to commence. As sheep farming grew on the main island of East Falkland, the populations of the striated caracara declined, despite the potentially plentiful source of carrion in the form of sheep and lambs.

Unfortunately the bird's notorious inquisitiveness has led to its persecution and has sparked much misunderstanding and folklore. What has been described as the caracara's mischievous nature is a form of curiosity mixed with opportunism in its continual search for food. The interest in my rucksack, for example, has a parallel with the bird's investigation of a moulting elephant seal. Often a caracara will probe and pull at pieces of a seal's skin, looking for food. Until some ten years ago, bounties were officially paid on the beaks of these rare birds, because of their supposed depredation of sheep. I suspect that many immature Johnny ROOKS, being the most brash, still meet their end because of their persistence in trying to balance on a radio mast and steal its brightly coloured piece of insulation tape, or in trying to ride a clothes line in a strong wind and seeming to take great interest in items of apparel.

West coast of New Island with rockhopper penguins coming ashore

The numbers of striated caracaras may also have been over-estimated. In March – the same month in which Darwin observed the species – numbers of dark-plumaged, immature birds, those more generally seen and described, disperse from their breeding sites. Settlements lying close to offshore island breeding grounds may attract these young birds, which scavenge about the sheep runs and 'haunt the neighbourhood of houses for offal', as Darwin observed. These young birds are especially curious about humans and this has led to the mischievous image popularly ascribed to the species as a whole. Beyond this, I have watched as many as forty birds scavenge about a single settlement, a sight that gives those unfamiliar with this species the impression of large populations. In fact, young birds from different breeding sites gather together to form flocks, and groups of immatures disappear almost as suddenly as they materialise; many of them die in their first winter. The stronger, more aggressive ones may reach maturity, but only 2 to 3 per cent achieve adulthood, find the right niche in what is a specialist environment and breed successfully.

Following my introduction to the species on Beauchene Island it was to become apparent that the Johnny rook, contrary to general belief, was itself a specialist. Much of my research into the general ecology of the Johnny rook was to be carried out on Beauchene Island. Getting to, and living on, the island was often a logistic nightmare, but the lure was its large, isolated population of caracaras. This miniature ecosystem provides the species with the same conditions that prevailed before humans settled the Falklands. On the line where the tussock grass meets the perimeter of the island's main seabird colonies are the nesting territories of some sixty pairs of *Phalcoboenus*, an amazing density for such a small island, but one that has remained at a constant level since my first visit to the island in 1963. My work has shown that the striated caracara's complex feeding ecology is interwoven with the life of local populations of birds, mammals and invertebrates. The key to its feeding pattern is shifting food availability, seasons of plenty alternating with those of great scarcity.

In September the colony nesting areas, deserted since April, slowly fill with black-browed albatross. Prions return to nest burrows beneath the loose rock debris that covers parts of Beauchene Island. The homecoming of these species constitutes an influx of food for the Johnny rooks. Prions a small form of petrel are preyed on directly: pairs of caracaras having territories within the nesting areas of these petrels even adopt semi-nocturnal behaviour to prey on the prions as they return to their breeding grounds at night. Of the tens of thousands of albatross coming back to the island, only a very small percentage of weak, diseased and injured birds afford a supply of carrion, as do debilitated rockhopper penguins, which appear in the first few days of October after an absence of nearly six months. The density of the penguin colonies also results in some fatalities as the birds struggle to maintain territories.

When the populations of adjacent colonies of rockhoppers and albatross reach a peak in October, pairs of striated caracaras begin to defend their territory more tenaciously. Immatures are no longer tolerated and are forced out into neutral zones to scavenge and prey, generally as a group, well outside adult territories. Adults, as well as holding nest sites, guard well defined feeding areas immediately adjacent to their nests. All the nests in my study were placed so as to give the caracaras a commanding view of the feeding area. Nests were commonly built on the fringes of the tussock grass, the grass usually serving as cover. With prey species, such as penguins and albatross, nesting right up to the tussock grass perimeters, the caracara is presented with a larder literally at its doorstep, one that effectively comes to the predator rather than forcing it to expend energy in search of its prey.

Caracara breeding begins in the third week of October, when the first egg of a clutch of three is laid. Timing coincides with the main flush of rockhopper penguin egg laying. By late November, just as the first caracaras are hatching, female rockhoppers, after a period spent feeding at sea, return to the colonies and relieve the incubating males. This exchange of parental duties in the over-crowded colonies dislodges an extraordinary number of near to hatching eggs from the nests. Thus, at the critical stage when the newly-hatched caracaras require soft, high nutrient food, protein is served up in the form of developed penguin embryos.

Offshore tussock island with coastal fringe of nesting seabirds

As the young caracaras develop, the hatching of rockhopper penguins begins, followed by that of black-browed albatross. Rockhopper chicks are an important prey for the Johnny rook which, unlike many hawks and falcons, spends much of its time on the ground. As Darwin noted, caracaras 'run extremely fast, very much like pheasants'. This ground speed is used to advantage when the birds prey on young rockhoppers.

Young striated caracaras become independent by early February. Growing rockhoppers leave the rookeries for the sea, but numbers of dead young litter the now depleting colonies. Juvenile caracaras, which feed mainly on prions and other petrels, now have an opportunity to test their predation skills. Fully fledged petrels emerge from underground nest chambers and head for the sea, depriving the less skilled young Johnny rooks of ready rations. The majority turn their attention to the albatross. Normal, healthy albatross chicks are now too large for the striated caracara to overcome, but many of these will die before they are fully fledged and capable of leaving the colony in April. Still, for the caracara, the days of plenty are dwindling.

By midwinter, in June, the island appears lifeless; the once packed colonies lie quiet and desolate, a sea of mud and guano. The only obvious signs of the once teeming breeding ground are the pedestal-like, raised mud albatross nests and the remains of young birds. Mud-soiled young striated caracaras roam the deserted colonies, hungry for carrion. When the food surplus of the warmer months diminishes, scarcity controls the caracara population. Many young will die, unable to compete with the more aggressive individuals for limited food supplies. The more skilled adult birds and some plucky immatures home in on marine molluscs, the invertebrates of the tussock grass stands and groups of resident gentoo penguins. Gentoos feed at sea but continue to occupy roosting sites ashore. Although feeding of young gentoos has long been discontinued, these sites become littered with what appears to be regurgitated food, which the most resourceful caracaras exploit.

Two Falkland mammals, the southern sea lion and the fur seal, are vital to the striated caracara's winter well-being. These seals will often seek the higher ground and protective tussock grass in the winter months. Their excrement becomes a vital food source for the remaining caracaras. The few current breeding sites of the Falklands population of striated caracaras have associated colonies of both gentoo penguins and seals. Only the existence of these colonies, adaptable eating habits and the exploitation of every available resource can ensure the caracara's survival.

No records document the number of gentoo penguins breeding on the north coast of East Falkland when Darwin recorded the Johnny ROOK as common, but there is little doubt that there were many more than at present. Sea lions, now scarce along that coast, were also prolific. After sealing and settlement depleted these forms of wildlife, the caracara simply disappeared from the scene.

Gentoo Penguin feeding chick by regurgitation

4 The Interior and Mountain Regions

Profound disturbances in the Earth's crust from time to time culminated in orogenesis, the process of the formation of mountains. The early stage of this process is a down-warping of the crust and the formation of a sea-filled basin in which thicknesses of sedimentary rock accumulate. Later, the sides of these basins move inwards, the bottom moves up and the layers of sedimentary rocks caught up in this squeezing action are folded, slide over each other and pile up into mountain chains.

The Falkland Islands owe their existence to folding movements of sedimentary rocks of the Paleozoic and Mesozoic eras. This folding gave rise to three principal mountain ranges in the islands: the folds, which occur in a somewhat winding course, run across the lower northern half of the East Falkland mainland on an east-west axis, giving rise to the Wickham Heights on this island and on West Falkland to a range known as Byron Heights. A third range, known as the Hornby Mountains, also on West Falkland, runs parallel with the Falkland Sound, almost at right angles to the former two ranges.

Elevations have a general summit level of 457–609m (1,500–2,000ft), the highest elevation being Mount Usborne in the Wickham Heights, East Falkland, rising to a height of 705m (2,312ft). Mount Adam on West Falkland is the second highest elevation, reaching 700m (2,297ft).

Although there is no evidence to suppose that the Falkland Islands supported permanent glaciers, those mountains of the archipelago which rise over 609m (2,000ft) show evidence of localised glaciation.

The broad, dome-shaped form of Mount Usborne has on its north-east side pronounced corries with small glacial lakes or tarns at their bases. Around the exposed shoreline of these lakes are ridges made up of rock debris, as though some past force, such as a glacier, moved down the side of the dome gouging out the corries and pushing before it debris behind which the lakes formed. Similar evidence of glaciers and ice domes is also to be found on the Mount Adam, Mount Robinson and Mount Maria ranges on West Falkland, while other parts of the islands appear to have experienced only a periglacial climate.

In areas where the quartzites are relatively undisturbed by folding, such as the area of East Falkland, north of the Wickham Heights and the centre and south of West Falkland, a relatively small number of isolated hills rise from gently undulating plains unbroken by rocky ridges or outcrops.

In the region of Port Stephens and Albemarle at the southern end of West Falkland, many of the hills are formed into almost perfect spherical shaped domes, yet in complete contrast the area is also dotted by a series of upstanding rock formations cut and sanded into amazing shapes, with descriptive names such as the Three Crows, Cauliflower Rocks and The Indian Village. Spread across the side of a gently inclined landscape to the south of Port Stephens, the latter appear as a cluster of Indian tepees. Many formations stand like narrow stacks 6–9m (20–30ft) or more in height, in parts whittled away to form narrow waists on top of which the rocks may swell out, giving the whole formation a precarious and top heavy appearance.

The 'Anvil' Stack, south east Falkland

112

Mount Usborne with a small glacial lake below the summit

Lower slopes of Mount Adam at Hill Cove, West Falkland

The interior regions, a mosaic of buffs and browns against grey quartzite rock ridges. Wickham Heights, East Falkland

Walking amongst one such formation I found myself within the walls of a small castle. Even the battlement walls, with the thin strata deeply cut where soft layers had been eroded away, gave the appearance of a man-made structure in need of repointing with mortar. Within the walls the air was still with a low murmur of wind outside, creating an atmosphere which made it hard to believe one was not actually standing in an ancient fort created by some earlier civilisation.

The interior regions, isolated from the richer food sources found on the coastal areas are, in comparison, thinly populated by bird life. Many interior crags will have a resident pair of red-backed buzzards, turkey vultures or crested caracara, and the Cassin's falcon – a southern race of the peregrine – also nest and range over the more mountainous areas. Within the interior regions, the presence of a particularly fertile valley, stream or pond may also be influential in the establishment of small populations of upland goose, snipe and even yellow-billed teal. Passerine birds – thrushes, black-throated finches, red-breasted meadow-larks, tyrants and pipits – may also be found in niches amongst the hills and mountain ranges, but one may also walk over miles of interior with little sign of bird life.

Viewed from afar these interior regions present a mosaic of buffs and browns with here and there dashes of rust reds, deep and medium greens, all against the predominant grey of the quartzite rocks which break up the landscape. But, walk across this mosaic of different coloured vegetation and the pattern becomes an intricate maze of less dominant colours from a large variety of plants. In the early summer months of October and November, the warmer, drier slopes of some hills can be dotted with the small orange-yellow flowers of ladies slipper (*Calceolaria fothergillii*). Entire hillsides are festooned with the delicate nodding heads of pale maiden (*Sisyrinchium filifolium*). Particularly noticeable on a warm, still day, a rather strong sweet scent rises from certain moister areas of the hillsides but its origin may not always be obvious to the casual observer. In a low light such areas may appear to glisten from minute globules of moisture. Look more closely and these globules will be seen to be sitting on top of small red hairs protruding from a mat of glossy green leaves. Sundew (*Drosera uniflora*) is one of the Falklands' smallest plants but unique in that it is an insectivorous plant, the rather sickly sweet smell attracting small insects to the globules of sticky nectar.

Although generally not common, *Viola maculata*, with its delicate yellow flowers, can be found in some mountain regions. Often conspicuous, producing bunches of bright yellow daisy-like flowers, *Senecio littoralis* is an endemic species and although perhaps not as prolific as in earlier times, is another plant adding colour to the landscape.

The notes made by Cunningham (1866–9) on the vegetation he observed in the hills close to Stanley are interesting, as they do indicate that in the immediate area of the capital, where stock was not common, the vegetation has changed little:

On the hillside I observed several species of plants already recognised in the Strait, such as the 'Diddle-dee' berry of the Falkland Islanders (a species of *Empetrum*, at one time regarded as distinct from the *E. nigrum* of Europe, on account of the red instead of black colour of the berries, to which the Upland geese are very partial); as well as others which were new to me, such as the famous Balsam-bog *Azorella (Bolax) glebaria*; the Falkland Island tea-plant (*Myrtus nummularia*); and the Almond-flower of the

Short-eared owl (Asio flammeus) *in cinnamon grass*

116

Rockhopper penguins Eudyptes crestatus *coming ashore*

White grass in late evening light on East Falkland

Blechnum *fern in late summer*

Opposite (top):
Feldmark formation on the west coast of New Island

(below):
Interior of West Falkland. Mount Robinson range

colonists. The first of these plants has for a long period attracted the attention of navigators who have touched at the Falklands, and its appearance is so extraordinary that a casual observer would be most likely to refer it to the order *Umbelliferae* to which it truly belongs. Dr Hooker remarks that –

"In whatever portion of this country the voyager may land, he cannot turn his steps inland without seeing scattered over the ground huge, perfectly hemispherical hillocks of a pale and dirty yellow-green colour, and uniform surface, so hard that one may break the knuckles on them. If the day be warm, a faint aromatic smell is perceived in their neighbourhood, and drops or tears of a viscid white gum flow from various parts of these vegetable hillocks. They stand apart from one another, varying from two to four feet in height, and though often hemispherical, are at times much broader than high, and even eight to ten feet long. The very old ones begin to decay near the ground, where a crumbling away commences all round, and having but a narrow attachment, they resemble immense balls or spheres laid upon the earth."

These plants puzzled Pernety; he called them 'plante au vernis' and experimented with the gum believing it a form of varnish. Penrose (HMS *Penguin*, 1772) believed it at first to be the work of a mole, while many of the early colonists referred to them as 'misery balls' because the land on which the plants were generally found was so poor it supported little else. According to Cunningham, some inhabitants believed it to be a kind of fungus. Vallentin, a naturalist who visited the islands in 1901–2, made the observation that if the surface of the growth was damaged and rain lodged in the break, the plant decayed rapidly and would be destroyed within a few months. Today the balsam bog is still common, but not to be found as Hooker described it; perhaps, as Vallentin observed, because it is so easily damaged.

On the more exposed hilltops characterised by areas of clay and other mineral soils, dwarf shrubs, ferns and some grasses found on the lower slopes give way to cushion forming plants known as a feldmark formation. Lichens and algae are also common, clinging to the small rock debris which is often scattered on these hilltops, but the predominant vegetation is usually made up of cushion plants. Balsam bog (*Bolax gummifera*) is commonly found on these exposed hilltops, a situation which may have resulted in its earlier name of misery balls. Species of *Azorella*, forming hard cushions but smaller than balsam, are also common. Another plant which appears to be restricted to feldmark is *Valeriana sedifolia*. Although feldmark formations appear more commonly on the higher exposed elevations, they are not entirely confined to such. On New Island areas of feldmark appear on some warmer north facing slopes only a few hundred feet above the sea. Such areas are characterised by the cushion-forming *Valeriana* which dot the landscape in mid-summer with cushions of bright yellow flowers.

Of some of the other more common plant forms Cunningham wrote:

The Falkland Island tea-plant is a little species of myrtle, the stems of which, thickly covered with small glossy leaves, creep over the surface of the ground, and has derived its name from having been frequently used as a substitute for tea by sealers who have visited the Islands. Its flowers are of a pinkish-white tint, and the fruit which succeeds them possesses an agreeable sweetish taste. The Almond-flower, so called from the delicious fragrance of its pretty white blossoms, which are succeeded by dark purple berries, belongs to a genus generally referred to the order *Liliaceae*. In the Falkland Islands I, as a rule, found it clustering in crevices of rock; but in the western part of the Strait it principally occurs half buried in moss at the base of the trees.

One of the most remarkable features of the Falkland Islands is the vast accumulation of rock which may cover large areas. These accumulations have acquired such descriptive names as 'stone runs', 'streams of stones' or 'stone rivers'. Pernety was the first to describe this geological phenomenon, believing it to be the result of some extreme earthquake. Pernety came across one of the largest stone runs, lying south-west of Berkeley Sound, which he named 'the great valley of fragments' and today goes by the name of Princes Street stone run. Like Pernety, Darwin, nearly sixty years later, concluded that the stone runs were of volcanic origin and wrote:

> We may imagine that streams of white lava had flowed from many parts of the mountains into the lower country, and that when solidified they had been rent by some enormous convulsions into myriads of fragments.

Queen Victoria Peak, New Island

Both Pernety and Darwin were incorrect in their theory of the origin of these stone runs, although the latter naturalist's description of these accumulations in my view remains a classic:

In many parts of the island the bottoms of the valleys are covered in an extraordinary manner by myriads of great loose angular fragments of the quartz rock, forming "streams of stones." These have been mentioned with surprise by every voyager since the time of Pernety. The blocks are not waterworn, their angles being only a little blunted; they vary in size from one or two feet in diameter to ten, or even more than twenty times as much. They are not thrown together in irregular piles, but are spread out into level sheets or great streams. It is not possible to ascertain their thickness, but the water of small streamlets can be heard trickling through the stones many feet below the surface. The actual depth is probably great, because the crevices between the lower fragments must long ago have been filled up with sand. The width of these sheets of stones varies from a few hundred feet to a mile; but the peaty soil daily encroaches on the borders, and even forms islets wherever a few fragments happen to lie close together. In a valley south of Berkeley Sound, which some of our party called the "great valley of fragments" [after Pernety], it was necessary to cross an uninterrupted band half a mile wide, by jumping from one pointed stone to another. So large were the fragments, that being overtaken by a shower of rain, I readily found shelter beneath one of them.

Their little inclination is the most remarkable circumstance in these "streams of stones." On the hill-sides I have seen them sloping at an angle of ten degrees with the horizon; but in some of the level, broad-bottomed valleys, the inclination is only just sufficient to be clearly perceived. On so rugged a surface there was no means of measuring the angle; but to give a common illustration, I may say that the slope would not have checked the speed of an English mail-coach. In some places, a continuous stream of these fragments followed up the course of a valley, and even extended to the very crest of the hill. On these crests huge masses, exceeding in dimensions any small building, seemed to stand arrested in their headlong course: there, also, the curved strata of the archways lay piled on each other, like the ruins of some vast and ancient cathedral.

Undoubtedly the stone runs and their formation present the most controversial feature in the geography of the islands. A number of theories have been put forward, although the generally accepted one is that the accumulations followed a period of freeze-thaw weathering in peri- or sub-glacial conditions. Before and during this period the present mountain ranges (built of alternating hard and soft layers of quartzite) would have been much higher, probably steep-sided towers of rock. Weathering of the softer layers by the freeze-thaw conditions crumbled these peaks and towers, producing the rocky debris which makes up the stone runs we see today, the actual positioning or transportation of such debris, often some miles from what is believed to have been their original location, being carried out by a process known as solifluction (the movement of wet soil or mud down a slope). This mud, derived from the softer rocks breaking down, acted as the vehicle for the transport of the harder blocks of quartzite.

Today air travel presents us with a bird's eye view of this geological phenomenon and an advantage over earlier investigators who puzzled over the formation of these rivers of stone. From the air it can be seen how the stone runs lead to the remnants of one time peaks, even to the extent that, like the pieces of some enormous jigsaw, it can be seen clearly where certain rocks fitted into the remaining outcrops. On one of the larger Jason islands, where perhaps periglacial conditions persisted, the mountain tops retain much of what appears to be their original form. Nevertheless it can be seen that the tips of the peaks have broken away and the resulting debris has formed miniature stone runs.

Grey quartzite ridges with their peaks broken away to form 'stone runs'. East Falkland

On Shingly Mountain on West Falkland the impression is that stone runs are still in some early form of development. On the slopes of the mountain, rocky debris has created waves of material across the slopes in much the same manner as the sea may form ripples on a sand beach.

When viewed from the air, many of the larger accumulations, especially in the Wickham Heights, show a more common but distinct pattern in the manner the rocks lie; yet viewed at ground level they appear as an irregular jumble of rock debris. These patterns disclose some interesting comparisons: the results of the way in which a water course, or the movement of a tide, grades out different sized particles of sand has similarities with these stone runs. Slow down these forces over millions of years and the process of solifluction starts to emerge. But could there have been variations?

On the higher elevations where there is evidence of glaciation and formation of ice domes, it is possible that some of the more extensive stone runs were transported by a modified process of solifluction. As the ice domes and glaciers receded one might visualise the higher rock towers and peaks gradually exposed and protruding out of a mantle of ice which, like a cape, surrounds the shoulders and slopes of the mountains. With the freeze-thaw conditions, the process of breaking down the now exposed peaks commences and solifluction starts, but on the surface of an ice sheet. In this manner rock debris could have been moved over much larger areas and, as the underlying ice sheet melted and the debris settled, the patterns we see in many stone runs may have been formed.

The stone runs themselves create another niche, especially for vegetation. Where soil and fine material has choked sections of boulder field and plants have eventually established, long thin islands of vegetation fleck the stone runs. Effectively isolated from stock, these islands offer the botanist an interesting assemblage of plants. Plants which are dwarfed and stunted on the more exposed surfaces of the *camp* grow lush and to a far greater size in the shelter of the boulders. On the slopes of the hill ranges, or where the present country-side has an underlying layer of rocky debris creating well drained conditions, beds of the fern *Blechnum magellanica* create a changing spectacle of colour. In the late spring and early summer new growth unfurls to cover large areas of the hillside in a deep, reddy brown. Gradually the fronds go through colour changes of orange, yellow, bright green, deep green and then finally, at the end of the growing season, turn a rich brown.

Apart from the very large number of streams which originate in the mountain regions, there are a number of rivers on West and East Falkland, all with their tributaries beginning in the higher interior regions. On West Falkland the Warrah River, which is about 18km (12 miles) long, is fed by a number of tributaries and small feeder streams that flow from the Mount Maria, Mount Robinson and Mount Edgeworth ranges, all of which enclose the river's course across the Warrah plain. The second main river on this island is the Chartres River with a length of some 25.5km (17 miles). It has many tributaries, with its main source rising in the Hornby Mountain range.

Two freshwater fish indigenous to the islands, native trout (*Aplochiton zebra*) and the locally named minnow (*Galaxias maculatos*) a form of smelt, can still be found in some rivers, but the introduction of an exotic species, the brown trout (*Salmo trutta*) in the 1940s has been largely responsible for the disappearance of these two species in many rivers and streams.

Mountain region. The Black Tarn corrie on Mount Usborne, East Falkland

124

Late evening on an offshore tussock island

Diddle-dee or red crowberry Empetrum rubrum *with* blechnum *fern*

The flowers of scurvy grass (Oxalis enneaphylla) *with mountain berry* (Pernettya pumila)

On East Falkland the San Carlos River, which has one of the largest watersheds in the islands, commences on the flats below Mount Usborne, with one of its main tributaries rising from the Black Tarn, the largest of the corries beneath the summit of this mountain. From source to mouth the river is about 45km (30 miles) long.

Although several other minor rivers exist on both East and West Falkland, the only other river of significant size is the Arroyo Malo or Malo River. The main sources of the Malo start on the north slopes of the Wickham Heights, the river running for a distance of some 22.5km (17 miles) with its estuary on the upper reaches of Port Salvador.

Where rivers flow across valley floors and their meanders have formed oxbow pools or shallows of relatively still water, niches are created for wildfowl and other water-loving birds. Most rivers support populations of both Rolland's and silver grebe, while yellow-billed teal, silver teal and Chiloe widgeon inhabit the shallow vegetated pools created by abandoned meanders.

Probably due to occasional flooding and subsequent deposition of alluvium and decaying vegetable matter, some lowland areas bordering rivers and streams are of a higher fertility than comparative land elsewhere. Such areas are often covered with dark green turf dominated by the native rush (*Juncus scheuzerioides*) and with large clumps of brown swamp rush (*Rostkovia magellanica*) frequently bordering the inland edges.

In some moister areas, along the banks of streams and covering the floor of some deeper valleys, grows one of the islands' larger shrubs. From a distance stands of this shrub produce a soft, grey-green colouration to the *camp*, turning almost white when it flowers in the late summer. Clayton, who landed at Port Egmont on Saunders Island in March 1773, referred to this as wild myrtle, an evergreen, 1.5m (5ft) in height and at that time in full bloom. This was fachine or fachinal bush (*Chiliotrichum diffusum*). When Hooker visited East Falkland in 1842 he referred to the fachine as a 'white flowered aster-like plant about four feet high' and being the most common shrub of the *camp*. In the early 1900s Vallentin wrote: 'In many valleys Fachina bushes abound and grow to considerable size from four to six feet high', but also mentioned that the plant was not nearly as plentiful as in earlier days, being 'quite useless' in the eyes of the sheep farmers and therefore having been ruthlessly destroyed. Today this beautiful shrub is common to some specific areas where it may still be found growing 0.9–1.2m (3–4ft) high, but in many areas there remain only small, stunted plants to indicate the extent of this shrub before stock was introduced to the islands.

Due to the rather selective grazing of sheep undoubtedly many other plants have been destroyed, but hopefully not completely annihilated. For me one of the most attractive areas in the Falklands is the range of hills which runs from an area overlooking Port Purvis through to Byron Heights. On its northern aspect numerous valleys with fast flowing streams run down to meet the various seaways which lie between this region of the West Falkland mainland and offshore islands such as Pebble Island, Keppel Island and Saunders Island. Unlike their counterparts on the south-facing slopes of the range, these valleys take full advantage of the northern sun. They appear warm and the vegetation looks richer. The beds of streams run over rock debris of a light, rust red colour, the whole creating a very colourful aspect.

A number of the older islanders can remember being told of a blue butterfly that was once common in this area. Some can recollect having seen the creature themselves and still there are very rare sightings of it. Hopefully, somewhere in one of these sheltered valleys there grows the remnants of some species of plant on which the missing butterfly may still cling to survival.

A species of butterfly which is fairly common to certain parts of the islands both on the West and East Falklands is the Queen of the Falkland fritillary (*Issoria cytheris cytheris*). As in the case of the missing blue, the host plant for the fritillary is unknown. I have watched adults feeding off a variety of flowers and on one occasion watched several dozens of these bright orange-red and black butterflies flying about a meadow where gorse was in flower. It may even be that such plants, introduced by man, are benefitting this species, for Vallentin, writing of the species at the turn of the century, indicated that it was restricted to the West Falkland.

Another butterfly which is not uncommonly observed making its swift zig-zagging flight across the *camp* in the latter half of the summer is the Southern painted lady (*Cynthia carye*). Closely related to the celebrated painted lady (*Cynthia cardui*), one of the most cosmopolitan migratory butterflies, this southern race is restricted to South America but amazingly makes its way to the Falkland Islands.

s Lowlands and Plains

East Falkland, south of the Wickham Heights range of mountains is almost severed in two by seaways: the Choiseul Sound entering from the eastern side and a smaller seaway, Brenton Loch, entering on the west side from the Falkland Sound. These two seaways are prevented from joining by a narrow waist of land at Darwin and Goose Green. This narrow isthmus effectively forms a land bridge and entrance to the large plain of Lafonia, the largest in the islands and one that composes roughly a quarter of the total land area of the Falkland Islands. Undisturbed by the folding which created the island mountain ranges, this plain rarely rises more than 30m (100ft) above sea level. Looking across it the eye travels over miles of low, gently undulating landscape, higher elevations being broken only occasionally by small outcrops of grey quartzite rocks.

The vegetation is largely composed of white grass (*Cortaderia pilosa*), which Charles Darwin described as 'a wiry grass of a monotonous brown colour'. Here and there, where a slight rise in the ground produces drier soil conditions, the predominance of white grass is broken by patches of dwarf heaths. Diddle-dee or red crowberry (*Empetrum rubrum*) is the most common of these, showing up dark green against the lighter coloured grassland. Among the more robust diddle-dee, two other dwarf heaths are often found, *Pernettya pumila*, bearing bright red berries, and Christmas bush (*Baccharis magellanica*) so named because of its fine yellowy-white flowers which appear in late December.

Travelling over this gently rolling *camp* there is at first glance no apparent shelter but then, quite unexpectedly, one meets numbers of low valleys, often with meandering streams running through them. The banks of these waterways support a rich growth of vegetation often dominated by the small tufted native rush (*Juncus scheuzerioides*), annual grasses and mats of pig-vine (*Gunnera magellanica*), all creating ribbons of rich green across the country.

In contrast to the coastal regions, the plains do not support a great deal of bird life. Small numbers of upland geese graze the valley floors and the large numbers of ponds which break up the area support waterfowl. The area also has its small population of raptors. Red-backed buzzards have their niche and curiously, due to the lack of rocky outcrops where they would normally nest, they have in some cases chosen man-made sites by utilising rolls of old sheep fencing on which to build nests.

From the writings of early naturalists and others who described these areas, there is little doubt that the vegetation, and to a certain extent the physical nature, of the plains has changed. The ground was described as being very soft, where snipe were so numerous that it was even possible to pick up birds by hand. Notes written by an unknown writer after a conversation with Mr Herbert Felton, one of the early farmers, give a vivid picture of one of the West Falkland plains:

The north of the island, Roy and Hill Cove, Port Howard, was covered with grass bogs reaching to under the knee; in between was fine grass and acres of celery. In many places this camp was difficult to get through. In 1871 a very fine summer the camp was fired and did enormous damage, burning the camp to the soil from Chartres to Port Purvis. It took fifteen years to recover, if it ever recovered properly. The blue grass was pulled up as soon as it tried to grow up (by the sheep) making the camp look like a hayfield. Stock kept fat winter and summer and the camp was always green. The White

A lowland and plain area on East Falkland. The lower slopes of the Wickham Heights appear in the background

grass camp as we know it was considered valueless. The best camps in Port Stephens were like this good camp. Cape Orford was only accessible along the beach at first. Felton shepherded the Merinos in South Harbour which was covered with bogs and grass. Cape Meredith was the same, and Calm Head. It took fourteen hours to reach Fox Bay and much walking had to be done.

Today few examples of such *camp* remain, much of the ground having been grazed down and consolidated. Flying over the plains and lowland areas one notices an amazing mosaic of lines crossing the *camp*. Only when it is realised that these denote sheep tracks does one become aware of how changes can occur. These changes, however, began more than 200 years ago, initially by cattle.

When de Bougainville's little expedition landed at Port Louis on East Falkland in 1764, they put ashore seven heifers, two bulls, some sheep, pigs, a goat, two stallions and a mare. These animals, taken aboard at Montevideo, were to be the forerunners of stock ranching which continues today.

Perhaps due to the softer, boggy nature of the ground and the lush vegetation which the country then supported, sheep do not appear to have fared well. The cattle, however, were to increase dramatically and in 1838 were estimated to number 30,000; by 1846 numbers had risen to 60,000. In the initial years following the introduction of this stock by de Bougainville, animals kept to the coastal areas where belts of the very palatable tussock grass grew but, as this diminished and the herds expanded, they moved inland to the smaller plains east of Salvador Waters and to the plains of Bombilla Hill and Chata Flats. Eventually groups of cattle made their way south along the edge of the Wickham Heights and then across the isthmus onto the Lafonia plain, where they increased to form some of the largest herds on East Falkland. Of these herds, Darwin recorded:

> The cattle, instead of having degenerated like the horses, seem, as before remarked, to have increased in size; and they are much more numerous than the horses. Capt Sulivan informs me that they vary much less in the general form of their bodies and in the shape of their horns than English cattle. In colour they differ much; and it is a remarkable circumstance, that in different parts of this one small island, different colours predominate. Round Mount Usborne, at a height of from 1000 to 1500 feet above the sea, about half of some of the herds are mouse or lead-coloured, a tint which is not common in other parts of the island. Near Port Pleasant dark brown prevails, whereas south of Choiseul Sound (which almost divides the island into two parts) white beasts with black heads and feet are the most common: in all parts black, and some spotted animals, may be observed. Capt Sulivan remarks that the difference in the prevailing colours was so obvious, that in looking for the herds near Port Pleasant, they appeared from a long distance like black spots, whilst south of Choiseul Sound they appeared like white spots on the hillsides. Capt Sulivan thinks that the herds do not mingle; and it is a singular fact, that the mouse-coloured cattle, though living on the high land, calve about a month earlier in the season than the other coloured beasts on the lower land. It is interesting thus to find the once domesticated cattle breaking into three colours, of which some one colour would in all probability ultimately prevail over the others, if the herds were left undisturbed for the next several centuries.

But the herds were not to be left undisturbed. Sealers and whalers who had begun to exploit the islands in the late 1700s had already found the cattle a very important source of fresh meat and during the period 1806–20, when the islands were abandoned by authority, these men hunted the cattle as and where they wished. When, in 1826, Louis Vernet obtained the fishing and cattle rights and established some ninety settlers at Port Louis, a significant

*Shipping produce
from an Island farm*

change was to take place in the hunting of cattle and on the plains where they were now to be found: Vernet's main income was derived from the sale of jacked beef, a form of dried meat, and cattle hides. In order to hunt the cattle efficiently, Vernet brought skilled horsemen in the form of *gauchos* from South America. Not only was a new style of hunting to be established, but the influence of the *gaucho* was to remain in other ways, as many of the names of areas in which they hunted signify: Cerritos Arroyo, Bombilla Hill, Campa Menta, Malo Hills, Laguna Legna and Dos Lomas House.

On the plains, where much of their lives were spent, these men became skilled in survival and in the art of living off the land. Darwin accompanied a group and wrote a vivid account of their life in the *camp*:

> The best fuel is afforded by a green little bush about the size of common heath, which has the useful property of burning while fresh and green. It was very surprising to seen the Gauchos, in the midst of rain and everything soaking wet, with nothing more than a tinder-box and a piece of rag, immediately make a fire. They sought beneath the tufts of grass and bushes for a few dry twigs, and these they rubbed into fibres; then surrounding them with coarser twigs, something like a bird's nest, they put the rag with its spark of fire in the middle and covered it up. The nest being then held up to the wind, by degrees it smoked more and more, and at last burst out in flames. I do not think any other method would have had a chance of succeeding with such damp materials . . .
>
> At night we slept on the neck of land at the head of Choiseul Sound, which forms the south-west peninsula. The valley was pretty well sheltered from the cold wind; but there was very little brushwood for fuel. The Gauchos, however, soon found what, to my great surprise, made nearly as hot a fire as coals; this was the skeleton of a bullock lately killed, from which the flesh had been picked by the carrion-hawks. They told me that in winter they often killed a beast, cleaned the flesh from the bones with their knives, and then with these same bones roasted the meat for their suppers.

As to the preparation of one such meal, he wrote:

> He cut off pieces of flesh with the skin to it, but without any bones, sufficient for our expedition. We then rode on to our sleeping place, and had for supper "carne con cuero", or meat roasted with the skin on it. This is as superior to common beef as venison is to mutton. A large circular piece taken from the back is roasted on the embers with the hide downwards and in the form of a saucer, so that none of the gravy is lost. If any worthy alderman had supper with us that evening, "carne con cuero" without doubt would soon have been celebrated in London.

The descriptions came back to me one day when I was journeying across an area of *camp* on East Falkland. Having stopped for a night's rest, I had chosen a small, sheltered depression on a slope facing north, thus taking advantage of the sun's warmth. As I settled down to camp I could well imagine the hardships these men endured, especially in conditions of high wind and rain. While preparing a meal, I wondered about the gauchos and their 'carne con cuero'. Cutting a square of turf under which I proposed to dispose of rubbish, I came across a layer of red ash. Probing deeper I exposed a number of beef bones and then to my amazement and delight a number of old hand-blown wine bottles. Although Darwin made no reference to wine being served with the 'carne con cuero', this had to be the site of an encampment used by *gauchos* over a hundred years ago, judging by the age of the bottles.

One of the most vivid descriptions of the actual hunting of the cattle is that written by Capt Grey some ten years after Vernet introduced his *gauchos* to the islands:

134

I wish I could only manage to give you a true description of the manner in which the wild cattle are caught; I have been out twice and can conceive nothing more exciting, hunting in England is not to be compared with it. I will endeavour to relate to you our last run which took place a few days ago; we set out from the settlement a little before eight, our party consisting of the French boy, the old Gaucho (Coronel), the Butcher, Smith and his son, besides myself and two of the Officers. We were all well mounted and the French boy leading, we struck into the interior of the island, riding over moors and bogs for some miles, nothing could be more dismal than the view – barren moors and bogs as far as the eye can reach without anything like a tree, in the bottoms there is a sort of shrub but our road today was to be the bleakest part of the island.

I was well mounted and resolved never to get the least in the rear, following the steps of the French boy and leaving it to my horse to choose where to cross the bogs. I had no difficulty in keeping up, but in crossing these boggy moors and traversing valleys, some with large and all with runs of water of some sort, in many instances, almost concealed by long grass. I could not conceive how it would be possible to catch the cattle, and cattle very different to those on the Pampas of Buenos Ayres which are to certain degree tamed, inasmuch as they are driven to a point every day, but the great difference is in the nature of the ground.

When we had been on horseback between two and three hours, the French boy broke the silence in which we had been riding for some time by calling out "Ganado" [cattle] and upon his pointing them out to me, I could at first only distinguish a black speck in the distance, not different to the bits of black bog which we had been constantly passing.

In a few minutes, I observed the speck to move, accompanied by four or five other specks; after a short consultation between the French boy and old Coronel, we began to make a sweep, the two dogs that were with us appearing to know that we had discovered what we were in search of, slunk close in behind the horses, and in this manner we made a detour of about a mile, when riding under a little hillock, the French boy dismounted and called upon me to do the same, creeping on our hands and knees we looked over into a sort of hollow beneath us, and as the French boy said "Aqui estan, señor" I saw within 500 yards of me four immense bulls, two feeding and two lying down, quite unconscious of our being so near them. I complimented the two directors of the good hit they had made and having remounted we prepared for the attack. Smith, his son and old Coronel were to go up one side of the valley, the French boy, the Butcher and myself on the other.

The lasso and balls (three stones about the size of your closed fist covered with hide and connected together by separate thongs of hide about six feet long, one ball is held in the hand and the other swung round the head and all three then thrown at the object with an aim and force that is astonishing) were prepared and lying along our horses backs, or rather hanging over the side away from the cattle, we sallied out in different directions from under cover of the hillock, and began to approach gently, stalking them as you would deer. The moment we appeared from behind our cover, we were discovered, but at first our approach being in a slanting direction did not frighten the cattle, we had not however got half way to them before the two that were lying down jumped up and all four dashing across the valley galloped towards the opposite hill.

The French boy observing this, put spurs to his horse and went off in pursuit of the bull nearest to us, followed closely by the Butcher and myself, being well mounted and determined to stick to my leader, I followed close, the chase leading us first of all over a boggy bottom where we crossed the stony bed of a brook and mounting the rise on the other side, we came up with the hindmost bull of the four. The French boy swinging the balls around his head threw them when we were about forty yards off with such precision, tangling about the bull's hind legs, down he came with a force to the ground that made the ground shake, when he kept floundering along and endeavouring to attack the dog that was now attacking him, the French boy seeing his beast disposed of, detached the lasso from his saddle and swinging it round his head, galloped off, shouting with excitement down a most tremendous bank after another victim. I pulled up here to see the first finished by the Butcher; Smith also joined us, his son and old Coronel having followed the chase in another direction. As the bull was limping along and trying to gore the dog that was flying at his lip, the Butcher after two attempts succeeded in throwing his lasso round his horns and then dismounting the well trained horse kept it tight while he, drawing out his long knife, went behind and hamstrung the poor beast, who fell down roaring with pain. The dog had now (having once been tossed) seized upon the bull's lower lip.

To my great disgust I found that the Butcher intended to leave him in this state without putting him out of his pain and when I expressed my surprise, his answer was that the hide would come off easier next day if not killed until then. I imposed my authority and whatever they might do on another occasion, I ordered him to kill him at once, which he did by going up behind as he lay on the ground and striking his knife into the spine where it joins the head. The poor beast was out of his misery in a moment. Leaving him and getting up the balls we rode after the French boy.

We found him about half a mile from us with an enormous bull lassoed and hamstrung which I caused also to be despatched, when he had succeeded in loosing this one, being quite alone, his life depended upon the steadiness of his horse, for dismounting, had the bull succeeded in extricating himself or in breaking the lasso which often happens, if not kept quite tight, he would then be with only his knife to defend himself against the infuriated beast. Brave as a lion and the most active lad I have ever seen, he had gone up boldly and brought his enemy down to the ground by cutting the sinews above the hock, which is called hamstringing.

In 1842 Governor Moody wrote of the large numbers of cattle to be found on East Falkland and the need to exploit them by a soundly financed company. In 1846 Samuel Fisher Lafone, a merchant of Montevideo, signed a contract with the government of the islands whereby under certain conditions he took charge of all wild stock on East Falkland. Lafone also purchased all the land to the south of the isthmus at Darwin, his hope being to establish a farming settlement. Lafone was never to visit the Falkland Islands, his operation being run by his agent, Williams.

On the south-east shore of Brenton Loch, at Hope Place, Lafone established an extensive *saladero*, or slaughterhouse and salting establishment. To prevent cattle escaping from the plain, Williams had his *gauchos* build a turf wall across the isthmus at Darwin and Lafonia itself turned into what was little more than a large slaughtering pen. Outside, the cattle were also ruthlessly hunted, Williams embarking on a wholesale slaughter largely for hides and tallow. Within five years it was reported that few cattle remained to the north of Darwin.

In 1860 the government resumed ownership of the wild cattle and issued a public notice to the effect that any person hunting cattle outside the plain of Lafonia without government permission would be fined. The precautions taken by the government to try and retain the remaining herds were insufficient. For sealers, whalers and the settlers, cattle killing became very profitable. In 1862 the newly formed Falkland Islands Company, which had purchased Lafone's failing business, was brought to court for killing cattle on Crown land. The company argued that the wild cattle were *ferae naturae*, an argument which was eventually upheld by the Privy Council. This decision was to seal the fate of the wild cattle and, although the government raised the fine for taking cattle illegally, they were slowly destroyed by the settlers.

Named after Lafone, the plain of Lafonia still retains some evidence of the great cattle herds that once roamed there. The stone ruins of the *saladero* at Hope Place can still be seen, as can a number of other remains which dot Lafonia. In the spring the eye is often attracted to small splashes of brilliant yellow against the landscape. Whether gorse was purposely or accidentally introduced is not clear, but it remains today as a very distinct marker of these older establishments, including the turf wall which runs across the isthmus at Darwin. Few dry stone wall corrals built in the cattle-hunting era remain, but

Mount Harriet, East Falkland in midwinter showing the typically thin snow covering on the higher elevations

136

the remains of many turf corrals are clearly evident from the air. Although broken down long ago their sites are usually marked by two circles of eroded ground, divided by a circle of vegetation, the latter indicating where turfs, stripped from the still exposed ground, were built up to form the wall.

On West Falkland a small plain is situated in the upper reaches of the Warrah River, embraced on its west side by Mount Edgeworth and Mount Robinson and to the south east by the Hornby Mountains. Until 1839 West Falkland had remained free of stock, but in that year Capt Sulivan, then Senior Commander of HM vessels in the South Atlantic, gave directions for cattle to be introduced to the island. In February 1839 sixty-six animals were landed at White Rock Bay, which has an entrance onto the Warrah River plains. Eighteen years later it was reported that between two and three thousand cattle roamed that area. Illicit cattle hunting, especially by sealers and whalers, was carried out on West Falkland, but these herds were largely left undisturbed until about 1867, when the island was officially opened to settlers.

The unknown writer referred to earlier again made some interesting notes concerning the cattle and settlement of the West Falkland:

> Port Howard was started first, followed by Shallow Bay and Port Stephens. When Port Howard was started thousands of cattle could be seen on the Plains. They were quite tame at first on seeing a man on horseback and would approach quite close. They would run from a man on foot owing to the sealers killing them. The cattle were magnificent and enormously fat. Three hundred and fifty hides were got in a week by three or four men.

No records exist of the breed of the original Falkland cattle introduced by de Bougainville but it is known that they had large, spreading horns. I have found remains of these in places where they have survived the elements and more than one *camp* house displays such spreads which have been handed down from the cattle-hunting days. The animals were also long haired, had broad fore limbs and small hind quarters, similar to the Spanish fighting breeds. Today no true wild cattle remain in the islands although curiously a small herd of such distinctive cattle remain on Volunteer Point, an area only a few miles from Port Louis, where de Bougainville landed the first cattle. These cattle have never in living memory been known to leave the point or to mix with other herds and it is, therefore, just possible that they are direct descendants of the original herds.

It was a calm, sunny day in February and I had walked to the point which guarded the entrance to the snug little Careenage harbour of Port Louis. On the point, protruding out of the closely cropped turf was the rear portion, or cascabell, of an old cannon. Firm and secure, it had been placed in the ground to form a bollard for mooring vessels. A few yards away, tucked into the side of the coast, were the dry stone remains of a building.

6 Settlement of the Islands

Reflecting on the position of the cannon-bollard, the remains of the building, the beach below and the sheltered harbour, I concluded that this was probably the spot on which, more than 200 years earlier, de Bougainville's small expedition had landed. From my position and looking back into the Careenage, I had a view of a low valley with a small, but fast flowing, stream running through it and into the harbour. This would have been the 'good and plentiful' supply of water recorded by Dom Pernety.

I decided that the high ground forming the side of the valley was probably where the party had first camped. One thing which had concerned them on landing was the complete absence of trees. Timber was essential for the future development of the colony they proposed, but it was also critical as a fuel for their immediate survival. Several shrubs were tried as fuel without success; it was Pernety, perhaps from his knowledge as a botanist, who conceived that the form of vegetation found here might produce a type of turf like that used in their native France. From the banks of the little stream by their camp Pernety dug a number of turfs and placed these about their fire; they had the satisfaction of noting that, on drying out, the sods burnt well. The discovery of peat as a fuel was in retrospect the most important finding and was to set the pattern of all future settlement in the Falklands. The sea, too, was to remain the islands' main road and therefore a sheltered harbour was of major importance. But many excellent harbours have remained unused because the development of a settlement was ultimately reliant on a suitable supply of peat.

Walking through Port Louis today it is still possible to find evidence of de Bougainville's original settlement. Here and there are the remains of a stone foundation or just a geometrical contour on a grassy paddock where a turf hut originally stood. On a rise, in semi-isolation, the remains of the fort erected by de Bougainville and his officers is still to be seen. The positioning of all these buildings is very irregular, and yet there is a pattern which developed from this very first settlement which can be traced to present day establishments.

Although a settlement today may differ in size from the small island farm with two or three houses, to larger mainland farms with twenty, thirty or even more houses, it will be placed near the coast usually at the head of a natural harbour. The principal dwelling or 'big house' still stands in semi-isolation but, with a new pattern now developing in farm ownership, the significance of these terms is changing. The other dwellings may be in closer proximity to each other but still detached, each with its peat stack and meat safe. Often a little distance away, perhaps taking advantage of a sheltered slope or valley, are the settlement gardens. Protecting each garden will be a wooden batten fence, more than one such fence constructed from oak barrel staves, a reminder of the days when supplies came to the islands in such containers. Although modern facilities are fast changing the pattern, most islanders, especially those living in the *camp*, show skills of improvisation. At the other extreme from garden fencing, I have seen beautifully designed chairs made from oak barrel staves.

With wool production the main industry, every settlement has its wool or shearing shed with an array of drafting pens, as well as a unit of dog kennels housing the dogs needed to handle sheep.

Many a visitor to a farm has puzzled over the gibbet-like structure with its arrangement of blocks and tackle usually to be seen in the vicinity of the shearing shed or outhouses. Known here as a *palenkey* (from the Spanish *palenque* on which horses would be tethered) it is an important part of each settlement's butchery, where mutton, or especially beef, carcasses are dressed and hung. Many households now have freezers for storing food, but the old and proved method of leaving carcasses of beef hanging outside is still preferred. Hung in this way, with fresh cuts taken off as required, meat will keep for one or two weeks in the cooler winter months.

Like any other rural community, those islanders living in the *camp* have learnt and handed down a number of traditional skills in living off the environment about them. Sealers and whalers of the late eighteenth century tried, often from necessity, many forms of bird life, eggs, plants and berries as food. A number of these developed into traditional foods, the colonists refining their use. The upland goose became one of these and remains a favourite dish. At Christmas time, the austral summer season, roasted upland goslings take the place of more traditional fare in some homes.

The eggs of penguins and albatross were discovered by early whalers and sealers as an important addition to their diet. In 1836 Capt Grey wrote:

> The sealers eat their eggs and so did many on board the *Cleopatra*. I never even had the courage to taste one; the American whalers have had some thousands of eggs buried in the sands, which are preserved fresh in this manner if buried when quite new laid.

Edmund Fanning, who made a number of sealing voyages to the islands (1792–1832) described his own discoveries as follows:

> The albatross begins to lay its eggs about the tenth of October; these are somewhat larger than those of a goose, having a shell of a dull white, the yelk being yellow, and if well cooked, makes a good dish for the table. The shag's eggs are speckled, with a blood-red yelk, and are not good for eating, having a strong fishy taste. The eggs most preferred of all that the South Sea country produces, are those of the Mackaronie penguin. This noble bird commences its laying during the first part of November: I have never known their eggs to be obtained at this rookery earlier than the second day of this month. These are a size larger than those of our domestic ducks, with a white shell, and much stronger than theirs; the substance being a little of the light blue cast, with a yellow yelk slightly tinged with crimson. They were always preferred by the officers; so much so, that while the ship lay here some were frequently served up at the cabin table with those of the common hen, cooked in different ways, and invariably selected on account of their superior flavor, and not being so dry as the hen's.
>
> I have kept these penguin's eggs in a good state of preservation, on board ship, for a period of nine months, by first immersing them in seal oil, though any will answer, then packing them in a cask with dry sand; a layer of sand, then a layer of eggs, and so on until the cask is filled, placing them all on their sides, with one end towards the bung, then heading the cask up, and stowing it bung up, in such a place as it can be got at on the third day, in order to be turned bung down, and so on; being turned every third day, until wanted for use, this method keeps the yelk from settling to the shell, and the sand mixing with the oil, forms a crust of sand and oil over it, by which the shell is kept perfectly air tight, and thus the egg is preserved from destruction.

The hazards of small boat work in the Islands

140

This custom of collecting eggs continued with the settlers developing it into an annual tradition. Until thirty years ago, several local vessels were employed in collecting large numbers of penguin and albatross eggs, both for use in the rural communities and for sale in Stanley. In the case of the latter, small boats, their holds full of eggs, would arrive after an egging trip at the public jetty, where the eggs would be sold. Today the tradition of egging remains, but has greatly diminished. There is no commercial collection of eggs and in comparison with earlier days, few eggs are sent to Stanley. But it is still possible to sit down to a breakfast table in a few *camp* houses and be offered a fried penguin egg or a boiled albatross egg, the latter so large that a teacup takes the place of the conventional eggcup.

Several species of wild berry are still collected and either eaten raw or made into preserves. The collection of these can be traced to the days of whalers and sealers. Fanning wrote: 'Of berries, there is a great variety, and in the proper season, large quantities may be collected. These we either ate raw, or made into puddings.'

One of the most popular berry collected in mid summer is that locally known as wild strawberry (*Rubus geoides*) which, in fact, is a small ground-hugging plant of the raspberry family. In the austral autumn months of March and April large areas of the *camp* can be covered with the small dark red berry of diddle-dee (*Empetrum rubrum*). Referred to as red crowberry by early voyagers, the fruit is still popular amongst many of the islanders. Making an excellent jelly preserve, it is served either as a jam or as a condiment with roast goose.

Another fruit still traditionally collected is the tea berry, although its use has changed. In 1836 Capt Grey referred to this as the 'Malvina tea plant', being

> a small green herb that grows in the ravines which, when boiled, makes a sort of stuff which resembles tea very much and although I cannot go as far as Capt FitzRoy, who says that he has given it to people without their finding out, yet it forms so good a substitute for tea that the men employed in the fisheries are quite content to have it served out to them.

Some years later, Cunningham wrote of the plant and also of the berry:

> The Falkland Island tea plant is a little species of myrtle, the stems of which, thickly covered with small rounded glossy leaves, creep over the surface of the ground, and has derived its name from having been frequently used as a substitute for tea by the sealers who have visited the Islands. Its flowers are of a pinkish-white tint, and the fruit which succeeds them possesses an agreeable sweetish taste.

Today the berries are commonly eaten raw, or go into cakes, but the use of the plant's leaves was not continued after the advent of the early sealers and whalers.

Scurvy grass (*Oxalis enneaphylla*) was found by early mariners to be rich in ascorbic acid and eaten raw or boiled was used to prevent scurvy. Wild celery (*Apium australe*) was also commonly used as a vegetable and as Fanning relates:

> In addition to what has been specified, there is another article of food, and this is the root [in fact the lower stem] of the coarse tussock grass which, when pulled up, breaks off close to its fibres; after taking off the outside cover, there remains a pulp about the size of ordinary sparrow-grass which on being eaten, tastes very much like a green chestnut, and is very nourishing.

142

Mutton, still a mainstay in many islanders' diet

In my travels about the islands I have frequently used wild celery and tussock grass stems to supplement a camping diet, while scurvy grass and sorrel I found to be useful thirst quenchers. Today, however, the excellent gardening skills of most islanders have long since taken over the need to use such plants. Reporting in 1842 Governor Moody wrote of the gardening potential:

> Of the cultivated vegetable productions, turnips, cabbages of all sorts, lettuces, radishes and potatoes grow to great perfection, especially the first. The swedes grow remarkably well and give an abundant crop. I have scarcely anywhere in England seen turnips to equal them, certainly not to surpass them.

Today these vegetables remain the main crops of most gardens, although the variety of vegetables grown has greatly increased.

When Moody made his report, cattle were still the main source of meat. Of the beef he wrote: 'The beef is fine grained, firm, and exceedingly well flavoured, and when cut from a wild animal in the interior, fat; particularly when there is tussock in the neighbourhood of their grazing ground.'

At the present time meat remains, for the majority of islanders, the most important item of diet, although the type has changed. With the development of sheep farming and the decline in the use of cattle, beef was replaced by mutton as the mainstay. So commonly is it used, especially on the *camp* settlements, that it has been given the name of '365'!

Curiously, the islanders have never turned to the surrounding seas as a source of food. Perhaps due to their more rural origins, fishing has never developed further than some inshore methods using rod and line, sweep net or the old but proved method of a 'fish wall'. Fanning described such a system:

> By raising a dam across near the mouth, of the rivulets and streams, and leaving a gateway that may be stopped at high tide, that excellent fish, the mullet, can be obtained in great abundance: they are equal, in my belief, to anything of the kind that the world can produce.

The remains of old fish walls, perhaps dating back to the days of Fanning, are still visible in some of the more remote coastal regions and many settlements retain a permanent wall across some nearby creek, the occasional catch being advertised by the appearance of gulls.

The almost predominant winds which blow across the islands have tested the endurance and spirit of many. For the gardener there is a continual battle against this element, yet I suspect that settlement of the Falkland Islands may not have been maintained without these winds. The warmer, drier winds which prevail from the westerly arc, especially during the summer months of October to February, are very important. At this period two very important tasks, the shearing of sheep and cutting of peat, essentially rely on these warmer winds. Sheep caught in rain or early morning mists dry out quickly in the high wind conditions, thus enabling shearing to continue with a minimum of lost time. Peat, still the most important fuel, can only be cut when these drying winds commence. In late September and October, the equinoxial period, when there is a tendency for stronger warmer winds to prevail from the west, peat cutting also starts.

Normally every household has its peat bank, an area in the *camp* allocated specifically where a person may cut peat. Flying over some earlier settlement areas shows that the pattern of peat cutting, even from the earliest times, appears to have changed little. The older peat banks are identified as square depressions in the *camp*, where a cutter appears simply to have cut out a square section of peat from a hole several feet square and a few feet deep, depending on the thickness of the deposit. The following season, the cut extended out on all four sides, or a new one was started. Shortly after, the method developed was to cut from a trench 1m (1yd) deep, 1m (1yd) wide and 137–182m (150–200yd) long. Each season a further strip of the same size would be cut from one or both sides of the trench.

Cut with a sharp-edged spade, a series of even-sized sods or turfs are removed from the side of the bank and tossed up onto the top surface. Watching a good cutter is like watching a precise piece of machinery, each 'yard' of peat being removed in the form of an exact number of sods, each of the sods being placed in order on the bank. When removed, the peat is soft, wet and black, but in the drying winds it quickly develops a hard crust on the exposed surfaces. As the sods dry and harden they shrink. The peat is then 'rickled', each sod being turned and placed into small heaps, thus allowing the unex-

Hand shearing

144

Cutting peat on the Stanley peat banks

posed sides to dry out further. It is then carted, these days usually by tractor and trailer, to the household's peat stack. Although perfected in some ways, the cutting and use of peat has changed little from the day when Pernety cut those first turfs. I often wonder if he realised then just how significant his find would be to the whole future of settlement in the islands.

When de Bougainville established the first settlement at Port Louis, buildings were either constructed from turf or a mixture of dry stone and clay, with tussock grass used as a form of thatch for the roofs. For over seventy years this pattern in building continued. In early 1840 Lt Tyssen, superintendent at Port Louis, reported that the majority of the inhabitants, still numbering less than twenty, lived – and preferred to live – in houses constructed of turf. John Bull Whitington, who arrived later that year, brought with him what was probably the first timber house in the islands. Described as a large dwelling with store rooms, domestic rooms and an office, the entire building accommodated eleven people. Falkland House, as it was named, was the forerunner of timber buildings in the islands, a pattern both in construction and design which is still common. Many of these earlier dwellings appear to have been clad with wooden shingles or lapped boarding, perhaps a mixture of influences from American sealers and whalers, whose homes on the east coast of North America would have been clad typically with shingles, together with some of the more common English styles of that period.

Long before the close of the 1800s, corrugated iron had become a popular form of roofing. It was introduced as early as 1847 and is still dominant today as a design feature on the majority of island buildings. Painted bright colours, these roofs add a splash of colour to the landscape and although contrasting greatly with the more subtle natural colours of the islands, the effect can be very pleasing to the eye. Although the basic design of houses has seen little change through the years, their adornments have, especially in the settlements. Aerials are now attached to most houses and on still, warm days when windows and doors are thrown open, bursts of radio transmitter conversation carry through the settlement. The radio transmitter has long been a means of communication for the more isolated settlement or shepherd's house but with the advent in recent years of the 'two-metre' radio net its use has extended to a point where most individual households in the *camp* and many in Stanley have such sets with which to keep in touch with each other.

Although the sea has remained the main road for the majority of settlements, with major requirements and produce moving by boat, tracks are an essential part of communications between settlements. Original routes laid out by early settlers still exist, although many are little more than beaten tracks meandering over the countryside, skirting stone runs, taking courses into seemingly impassable *camp* in order to link up a settlement or remote shepherd's house. Some are still trodden and marked by horses hooves and at certain times of the

Beaver float aircraft. Major form of transport until 1982

year, when the ground can become waterlogged, remain more easily negotiated on horseback, although the horse as a means of transport has generally declined. Motorbikes, Land Rover type vehicles and tractors are now used more extensively. The days when the inhabitants of several settlements embarked on a journey, all on horseback, for a social gathering at another settlement, perhaps more than a day's ride away, have all but gone.

In sharp contrast with an ability to overland by horseback or vehicle, often negotiating the roughest of terrain, the islanders must be at the same time one of the most modern travellers in the world. For the majority, more especially those living on the outlying islands, air travel has been commonplace for well over thirty years. For many years Beaver float aircraft served the islands, utilising as landing areas the harbours on which settlements are placed. Then, partly as a result of the 1982 conflict and the need for a more economical system, the service was changed and today Islander land aircraft are used. Based in Stanley, three such aircraft operate on an unscheduled basis, carrying passengers, mail and freight to some forty different settlement grass strips dotted about the archipelago.

Although the islands lie, at the closest point, only some 525km (350 miles) from their South American neighbour, the influence of immigrants from that continent was little. The *gauchos* and Indians found by Darwin and other early voyagers were not to remain in the islands for many years, yet they had a surprising influence in other ways which has continued. Many Spanish place names remain and although spelling and pronounciation may have been distorted from the original, Spanish terminology used by the *gauchos* is still commonplace, perhaps the most commonly used being *camp* from the Spanish *campo*, meaning countryside. Names for different items of horsegear, even the colour combinations of the horses themselves, are also of *gaucho* origin.

Although American whalers and sealers worked the islands for many years and adopted self-styled homes in a number of harbours on the west of West Falkland, they were to have little if any lasting influence on the islands' development.

Shortly after Moody's arrival in the Falklands with his small group of tradesmen colonists he reported back to Lord Stanley that:

> The settlers best adapted to colonise these Islands would be from among the industrious population of the Orkneys and Shetland Islands accustomed to a hardy life, and as much seamen as landsmen; but all settlers from grazing and sheep farming districts would find land and climate admirably adapted to the kind of farming to which they had been the most accustomed. Brickmakers, from the districts where bricks are burnt with peat, as in Huntingdonshire, would also be very useful.

Many colonists that followed Moody were in fact families from crofting communities of the Scottish Isles but equally, many were rural people from the southern counties of England.

Another significant aspect in the building up of the community was the influence of the government immigrant of which many, like Moody's party, were military men and their families. To add to the community pattern there were those immigrants who arrived as seafarers, remnants of shipwreck or perhaps sealing or whaling expeditions.

So it was that the foundation was laid for a community which over the years has moulded together to form an island person, basically a rural person but one with the added skills of a tradesman, resourceful and very adaptable.

An island teenager

Russian stern trawler

148

Epilogue

As we closed on Macbride Head and our angle of sight changed, the stern of a very large vessel slowly came into sight from behind the point. When some three to four miles from Macbride Head the vessel was easily recognisable as a whale factory ship. Her special superstructure of derricks, smoke stacks etc could now be seen. It was also quite clear that she was still at anchor and therefore we had a very good chance of making her position before she attempted to make a move out of Falkland waters.

When we were within one mile of the factory ship, a catcher suddenly appeared from behind it, heading away from our position and out to sea. The catcher was first sighted some thirty minutes before, when she was making for the factory ship. In that short time she had been alongside the mother ship, no doubt discarded her catch of whales and possibly refuelled. It was fairly obvious from her speed in each direction that she did not wish to be inspected by us. As we approached the factory vessel, I was asked by the Customs Officer if I would act as witness to the fleet's position, take photographs, and board the Russian factory ship in order to investigate further and deliver a protest at the fleet's whaling activities in Falkland waters.

In retrospect it was a ridiculous situation: one very small ex-motor fishing vessel with a total complement of six which included the customs officer and myself, against an entire Russian whaling fleet. A few hours later and only a few miles from the Russian vessels a whale appeared on our port beam and blew. It was the last whale I was to see alive in these waters. The date was 24 March 1962.

Some ten years later I was to write of another experience. Strangely it was this time a dream, a premonition of a happening in the distant future:

For more than four days now the trawler had been slowly moving from north to south and back again. On coming within a few miles of the island she would turn and make her way back, then later return again. Day and night she worked, at night her position being marked by the floodlights fitted on the back of her slipway. That I had bothered to climb to the top of the high cliff late at night, just to see if she was still working, was rather ridiculous, for I knew that such vessels, costing many thousands of pounds a day to operate, had to work round the clock. What nationality she was I had no idea, but I knew she would be collecting food for some protein-hungry nation. They would be working under licence; what many called "controlled fishing". But at whose expense? It was January, and we had been spending a lot of time on the rockhopper penguin colony trying to establish why the birds were getting later in their breeding cycle. One thing we had established was that the adult birds were now spending much longer at sea before returning with feed for their young. Had some biological change taken place in the food chains? Twenty years ago we would have said "Yes, very probably". Now the cause was staring us in the face. Some years ago all seal colonies in the islands had been declared reserves of special value; gone at last were the dangers from sealing. But owing to economic pressures the authorities had then issued larger catch quotas to the fishing fleets, extending these to include the forms of "krill" in the range of marine life that could be taken. Within a short space of time the fur seal population had fallen, and now the same was happening to the bird colonies. I was not sure which was worse: this slow starvation or the disaster we had witnessed the previous year, when one of the mammoth oil flubbers used for storing oil from the off-shore drilling bases had broken loose in a storm. There had been oil spills before, but this time several thousand tons of crude oil had been lost and tens of thousands of penguins, cormorants and albatross had perished.

Regrettably the dream has suddenly become reality. In less than ten years since I wrote, I sat on that same island and watched through the night as some fourteen trawlers went back and forth. During the day they remained some ten miles off, but at night they closed in on the island enabling me actually to see detail on their superstructure under their jigging lights. They are not after krill;

The author on remote offshore island

150

the quarry is squid, but the effect will be the same and another very important food of the islands' bird and seal populations is being taken.

While the Falkland Islands remained comparatively obscure and fairly isolated from the rest of the world, and its inhabitants were yet to be caught up in the fast moving wheel of that world, it seemed that the natural environment was becoming increasingly important and an integral part of life in these islands. The environment and its wildlife were attaining the recognition they deserved; gradually it was being realised that such things were now rare in the world and that this could be the greatest natural asset of the Falklands. Considerable strides were made in the islands towards conserving this asset and some thirty reserves had been created. Slowly but positively, specialised wildlife tourism developed and the message was being carried to the outside of a new and exciting untouched part of the globe. Such was the interest, that suggestions were even being made that the solution to the then rumbling question of sovereignty over the Falkland Islands could be found through its wildlife. Was it not possible, for example, that the islands could be turned into some form of international wildlife reserve, with the islanders as trustees. The options it appeared were many and not out of reach.

Then, dramatically, the islands were plunged into the 1982 conflict between Argentina and Great Britain and there have been changes. I am often asked what damage the actions of the war did to the environment; the answer is very little. The greatest threat of damage has come from the attention the conflict brought on the islands. The area became a focal point for the world; the islands were rediscovered and given a new importance. Following this has come aid and an overwhelming cry for the development of the Falklands.

While the islands remained a step or two behind they had the great advantage of learning from the mistakes of others in the outside world. The pace of progress was such that precautions could be taken to ensure adequate protection of the environment; today the pace is such that little time is available, it seems, for such matters. For me the whaling activity episode was my first experience and warning of the damage that man is capable of doing to this environment.

I believe the present experience involving the fishing fleets working off these islands is yet another warning.

This work I sincerely hope will present something of the very special and unique nature of these islands as they are today. I also hope that it conveys the message that the Falklands, 'Nature's Islands', have a very delicate and vulnerable ecosystem and only with man's care and due consideration will it survive not just as a great potential development asset to the Falkland Islands but as one of the world's greatest natural heritages.

Bibliography

Boyson, V. *The Falkland Islands* (Oxford, 1924)

Cunningham, Robert O. *The Natural History of the Straits of Magellan Made during the Voyages of HMS Nassau 1866–69* (Edinburgh, 1871)

Dampier, William. *A New Voyage Round the World* (1697)

Darwin, Charles. *A Naturalist's Voyage HMS Beagle* (1860)

Dodge, Bertha S. *MAROONED Being a Narrative of the Sufferings and Adventures of Captain Charles H. Barnard 1812–16* (Edited and with an Introduction by Bertha S. Dodge; Wesleyan University Press, 1979)

Fanning, Edmund. *Voyages and Discoveries in the South Seas 1792–1832*

Grey, Captain. Extracts from Diary, Voyage on HMS *Cleopatra*, 1836

Moody, R. C., Lieutenant Governor. Despatches and letters, Government archives, Stanley

Moore, D. M. 'The Vascular Flora of the Falkland Islands' *British Antarctic Survey Scientific Report No 60* (1967)

Pernety, Dom. *Histoire d'un Voyage aux Isles Malouines fait en 1763 et 1764* (1770)

Ross, Sir James. *A Voyage of Discovery and Research in the Southern and Antarctic Regions 1839–43* (1847)

Stackpole, Edouard A. *The Sea Hunters* (Lippincott USA, 1953)

Strange, I. J. *The Falkland Islands* (David & Charles 1972, 1981, 1983, 1985)
The Bird Man (Gordon & Cremonesi, 1976)
The Falklands: South Atlantic Islands (Dodd Mead, New York, 1985)
Penguin World (Dodd Mead, New York, 1981)

Weddell, James. *A Voyage Towards the South Pole 1822–24* (1825)

Chronology

1592 Islands discovered by Capt John Davis in the *Desire*

1594 Sighted by Sir Richard Hawkins, who named the islands 'Hawkins Maiden Land'

1600 Dutch navigator Sebald de Weert sighted and named the group of islands later known as the Jason Islands

1690 First undisputed landing by Capt John Strong of the *Welfare*

1701 Landing recorded by French navigator Gouin de Beauchene

1763/ 1764 French expedition led by Antoine Louis de Bougainville left St Malo on the ships *Eagle* and *Sphinx* carrying settlers and stores to establish a colony. Entered what was later named Berkeley Sound (East Falkland) in February 1764. A fort was built – Fort St Louis – and a ceremony of possession took place on 5 April 1764. The French called the Islands Iles Malouines, after the expedition's port of origin

1764/ 1765 A survey expedition comprising the *Tamar* and *Dolphin* left Britain in June 1764 led by Commodore John Byron. They arrived at Saunders Island (West Falkland) in January 1765. The harbour was re-named Port Egmont and Byron claimed the Islands for King George III

1765/ 1766 An expeditionary force was sent from England in September 1765 under the command of Capt John McBride with the frigate *Jason*, the sloop *Carcass* and the store ship *Experiment*. They reached Port Egmont in January 1766 and erected a shore establishment

The French settlement at Fort Louis was sighted by McBride's men in December 1766. McBride sent a letter to the French commander informing him of Britain's claim to the Islands. Both commanders unaware of France's transfer to Spain; (see below)

1766 October. France agreed to transfer the colony to Spain on payment of a sum equivalent to £25,000. Bougainville sailed once more to the Islands and his vessel was joined en route by two Spanish frigates; all reaching the Islands in March 1767

1767 On 1 April the Colony was formally handed over to Spain, M. de Nerville being succeeded by the Spaniard Felipe Ruiz Puente. Port Louis re-named Port Soledad

1769 Capt Hunt HMS *Tamar* meets up with Spanish. This eventually leads to confrontation of the small British force and overwhelming Spanish forces at Port Egmont. Under articles of capitulation the British surrender their settlement at Egmont

1770 British force leave Port Egmont and return to England

1771 Spain and Britain almost declare war over the incident but negotiations result in an order for restitution being signed 7 Feb, 1771. Later in 1771 the British again take over Port Egmont

1774 Britain abandon the settlement at Port Egmont

1806 The Spanish abandon the settlement at Port Soledad

1806 to 1820 Islands completely abandoned by all forms of authority
Whalers, sealers and privateers use the archipelago to their liking

1820 1 November. Formal rights of possession declared in name of newly created United Provinces of the River Plate

1823 First Argentine Governor of the Islas Malvinas appointed. In same year the United Provinces grant land and fishing rights to Louis Vernet

1828 Louis Vernet granted rights to entire East Falkland and in June 1828 appointed Governor of the Islas Malvinas

1831 Vernet's settlement at Port Louis sacked by United States corvette *Lexington* as reprisal for Vernet's attempts to stop sealing by North American vessels and his seizure of three such vessels

1832 Temporary Spanish Governor takes over Port Louis (Soledad). Shortly after he is killed by Spanish mutineers and confusion again reigns over the possession. The commander of the *Sarandi*, Jose Maria Pinedo, takes temporary charge
On 20 December 1832 HMS *Clio* Capt Onslow (despatched to take possession of the Islands) arrives at Port Egmont

1833 2 January. Capt Onslow aboard *Clio* unexpectedly arrives at Port Louis and issues Pinedo with a letter of his intention to 'exercise the right of sovereignty over these islands'. On 5 January Pinedo leaves aboard the *Sarandi* bound for Buenos Aires. Four days later Onslow departs leaving William Dickson, a British

1833	subject one time storekeeper for Vernet, in charge.
	March 1833 the *Beagle* commanded by Capt FitzRoy with Charles Darwin aboard visits Port Louis. During their visit Capt Matthew Brisbane, senior British resident, takes charge of the settlement.
	26 August 1833 Brisbane, Dickson and three other settlers attacked and murdered by lawless element of the Port Louis community
1834	HMS *Challenger* arrives at Port Louis. Lt Smith installed as Naval Superintendent and Governor.
1840	The Colonial Lands and Emigration Commissioners propose that the Islands be colonised
1841	On 2 August Richard C Moody appointed Lt Governor of the Falkland Islands
1842	On 15 January the *Hebe* with Moody aboard anchored at Port Louis and on 22 January he made his official landing informing the settlers that HMG would look after the Islands
1843	Work commenced on a new town site at Port William
1845	18 July. Stanley was officially recognised as the new capital and seat of government
1846	First large grant of land made to Samuel Fisher Lafone
1851	Falkland Islands Company formed
1854	Ship repair trade develops
1867	Ship repair trade at its height
1869	Entire land area of West Falkland leased for farming
1874	Occupation of the Colony officially returned as sheep farming
1914	Battle of the Falkland Islands
	On 8 December the British Naval Squadron under Admiral Sturdee defeated the German fleet commanded by Admiral Van Spee
1939	During World War II Stanley became an important Naval base and Radio Telegraphy station
1964	August. The inhabitants of the Islands told the United Nations Committee on Decolonisation that they wished to retain association with Britain
1968	March. Four unofficial members of the Islands Council appealed to members of Parliament in Britain to intercede to prevent the Government making an agreement with Argentina over the heads of the Island inhabitants
1971	Communications Agreement signed between Britain and Argentina. First direct communications link established between the Islands and Argentina
	Shipping link with Montevideo, Uruguay, ceases
1972	Stanley Airport (temporary airstrip, Argentine built) opens
1976	Lord Shackleton's Economic Survey of the Falkland Islands
1977	British built airport at Cape Pembroke opens December
	In resumed British–Argentine talks the question of a transfer of sovereignty was formally discussed
1980	In the period 22–9 November the Hon Nicholas Ridley MP Minister of State at the Foreign Office visited the Islands and spoke to Islanders about how the sovereignty dispute might be resolved
1981	Further talks held under the auspices of the U.N.
	The Islands Legislature called for a 'freeze' of the negotiations
1982	2 April. Argentine Forces invade the Falkland Islands
	1 May. British Task Force moved into Exclusion Zone
	Vulcan bombs Stanley Airport
	21 May. British Task Force lands at San Carlos, East Falklands
	14 June. Commander of Argentine forces surrender to Commander British Task Force
	Update of Lord Shackleton's 1976 Economic Survey published September
	December. Foreign Secretary outlines development plan to implement Shackleton Report and announces aid amounting to £31m
1983	January. Prime Minister Margaret Thatcher visits Falklands
	British firms are asked by HMG to tender for the construction of a new airport at Mount Pleasant
1985	12 May. New airport at Mount Pleasant officially opened by HRH The Prince Andrew
1986	November. Britain declares 150 miles Interim Fisheries Conservation & Management Zone around the Islands

Appendix

Selected List of Falkland Islands' Flora

Hymenophyllum falklandicum · Falkland Filmy-fern
Gleichenia cryptocarpa · Coral Fern
Rumohra adiantiformis · Leathery Shield Fern
Polystichum mohrioides · Falkland Shield Fern
Blechnum penna marina · Small fern
Blechnum magellanicum · Fuegian Hard Fern
Rumex acetosella · Sheep's Sorrel
Calandrinia feltonii · Felton's Flower (endemic)
Colobanthus quitensis · Pearlwort
Spergularia media · Sand Spurrey
Chenopodium macrospermum · Goosefoot
Caltha sagittata · Marsh Marigold
Ranunculus trullifolius
R. biternatus · Crowfoot
R. maclovianus
R. repens · Creeping Buttercup
Hamadryas argentea · Silver-leafed Ranunculus (endemic)
Drosera uniflora · Sundew
Arabis macloviana · Falkland Rock Cress (endemic)
Draba funiculosa · Whitlow Grass
Crassula moschata
Saxifraga magellanica · Fuegian Saxifrage
Rubus geoides · Native Strawberry
Acaena magellanica · Prickly Burr
Acaena pumila
Oxalis enneaphylla · Scurvy Grass
Viola maculata · Native pansy
Myrteola nummularia · Teaberry/Malvina berry
Myriophyllum eltinoides · Native Water-milfoil
Gunnera magellanica · Pig Vine
Azorella lycopodioides
A. filamentosa
A. caespitosa
A. selago
Bolax gummifera · Balsam-Bog
Lilaeopsis macloviana · (endemic)
Apium australe · Wild Celery
Pernettya pumila · Mountain Berry
Gaultheria antarctica
Empetrum rubrum · Diddle-dee
Primula magellanica · Dusty Miller
Anagallis alternifolia · Native Pimpernel
Armeria macloviana · Falkland Thrift
Gentianella magellanica · Native Gentian
Galium antarcticum · Antarctic Bedstraw
Calceolaria fothergillii · Lady's Slipper
Hebe elliptica · Native Boxwood
Euphrasia antarctica · Antarctic Eyebright
Valeriana sedifolia
Pratia repens · Creeping Pratia

Nastanthus falklandicus · (endemic)
Aster vahlii · Marsh Daisy
Erigeron incertus · (endemic)
Baccharis magellanica · Christmas Bush
Chiliotrichum diffusum · Fachine
Chevreulia lycopodioides · (endemic)
Gnaphalium affine · Falkland Cudweed (endemic)
Senecio candicans · Sea Cabbage
S. littoralis · Yellow Daisy (endemic)
S. vaginatus · (endemic)
Nassauvia gaudichaudii · (endemic)
N. serpens · (endemic)
Leuceria suaveolens · Vanilla Daisy (endemic)
Perezia recurvata · Falkland Lavender
Potamogeton linuatus · Native Pondweed
Astelia pumila
Enargea marginata · Almond Flower
Sisyrinchium filifolium · Pale Maiden (endemic)
S. chilense
Juncus scheuzerioides · Native Rush
Rostkovia magellanica · Brown Swamp Rush
Marsippospermum grandiflorum · Tall Rush
Luzula alopecurus · Native Woodrush
Poa flabellata · Tussac Grass
Poa alopecurus · Mountain Blue Grass
Poa robusta · Spikey Grass/Prickly grass
Festuca erecta · Land Tussac
Festuca magellanica · Fuegian Fescue
Agropyron magellanicum · Fuegian Couch-grass
Agrostis magellanica · Fuegian Bent
Deschampsia antarctica · Antarctic Hair-grass
Cortaderia pilosa · White Grass
Hierochlöe redolens · Cinnamon Grass
Alopecurus antarcticus · Antarctic Foxtail
Scirpus californicus
Isolepis cernua · Nodding Scirpus
Eleocharis melanostachys · Spike-rush
Carex fuscula
Carex trifida · Sword-Grass
Chloraea gaudichaudii · Yellow Orchid
Gavilea australis
G. macroptera
Codonorchis lessonii · White Orchid

Selected List of Kelps and Seaweeds
Macrocystis pyrifera · Giant Kelp
Durvillea antarctica · Giant Tree Kelp
Lessonia antarctica · Tree Kelp
Iridaea sp.
Ulva sp. · Sea lettuce

Checklist of Breeding Birds
King Penguin · *Aptenodytes patagonicus*
Gentoo Penguin · *Pygoscelis papua*

Rockhopper Penguin · *Eudyptes crestatus*
Macaroni Penguin · *Eudyptes chrysolophus*
Royal Penguin · *Eudyptes chrysolophus schlegeli*
Magellanic Penguin · *Spheniscus magellanicus*
White-tufted Grebe · *Podiceps rolland rolland*
Silvery Grebe · *Podiceps occipitalis*
Black-browed Albatross · *Diomedea melanophris*
Southern Giant Petrel · *Macronectes giganteus*
Thin-billed Prion · *Pachyptila belcheri*
Fairy Prion · *Pachyptila turtur*
White-chinned Petrel · *Procellaria aequinoctialis*
Greater Shearwater · *Puffinus gravis*
Sooty Shearwater · *Puffinus griseus*
Wilson's Storm-Petrel · *Oceanites oceanicus*
Grey-backed Storm-Petrel · *Garrodia nereis*
Falkland Diving Petrel · *Pelecanoides unrinatrix berard*
Rock Shag · *Phalacrocorax magellanicus*
Imperial (King) Shag · *Phalacrocorax (atriceps) albiventer*
Black-crowned Night Heron · *Nycticorax n. cyanocephalus*
Black-necked Swan · *Cygnus melancoryphus*
Ruddy-headed Goose · *Chloephaga rubidiceps*
Upland Goose · *Chloephaga picta leucoptera*
Kelp Goose · *Chloephaga hybrida malvinarum*
Patagonian Crested Duck · *Lophonetta s. specularioides*
Falkland Flightless Steamer Duck · *Tachyeres brachydactyla*
Flying Steamer Duck · *Tachyeres patachonicus*
Yellow-billed Teal · *Anas flavirostris*
Chiloe Wigeon · *Anas sibilatrix*
Brown Pintail · *Anas georgica spinicauda*
Silver Teal · *Anas versicolor*
Turkey Vulture · *Cathartes aura falklandica*
Red-backed Hawk · *Buteo polyosoma*
Striated Caracara · *Phalcoboenus australis*
Crested Caracara · *Polyborus plancus*
Peregrine (Cassin's) Falcon · *Falco peregrinus cassini*
Pied (Magellanic) Oystercatcher · *Haematopus leucopodus*
Black Oystercatcher · *Haematopus ater*
Two-banded Plover · *Charadrius falklandicus*
Rufous-chested Dotterel · *Zonibyx modestus*
Common Snipe · *Gallinago gallinago*
Great Skua (Antarctic Skua) · *Catharacta skua antarctica*
Dolphin Gull · *Larus scoresbii*
Dominican Gull · *Larus dominicanus*
Pink-breasted (brown-hooded) Gull · *Larus maculipennis*

South American Tern · *Sterna hirundinacea*
Short-eared Owl · *Asio flammeus*
Tussock Bird · *Cinclodes antarcticus antarcticus*
Dark-faced Ground-tyrant · *Muscisaxicola macloviana macloviana*
Grass or Marsh Wren · *Cistothorus platensis falklandicus*
Cobb's Wren · *Troglodytes aedon cobbi*
Falkland Thrush · *Turdus falklandii falklandii*
Falkland Pipit · *Anthus correndera grayi*
Long-tailed Meadowlark · *Sturnella loyca falklandica*
Black-throated Finch · *Melanodera m. melanodera*
Black-chinned Siskin · *Spinus barbatus*
House Sparrow · *Passer domesticus*

Checklist of Mammals

Pinnipeds: Sea Lions and Seals
Southern Sea Lion · *Otaria byronia*
Falkland Islands Fur Seal · *Arctocephalus australis*
Southern Elephant Seal · *Mirounga leonina*
Leopard Seal · *Hydrurga leptonyx*

Cetaceans: Whales, Dolphins and Porpoises
Pygmy Right Whale · *Caperea marginata*
Blue Whale · *Balaenoptera musculus*
Sei Whale · *Balaenoptera borealis*
Minke Whale · *Balaenoptera acutorostrata*
Fin or Finner Whale · *Balaenoptera physalus*
Southern Right Whale · *Eubalaena australis*
Humpback Whale · *Megaptera novaeangliae*
Sperm Whale · *Physeter macrocephalus*
Cuvier's Beaked Whale · *Ziphius cavirostris*
Arnoux's Beaked Whale · *Berardius arnuxii*
Layard's Strap-Toothed Whale · *Mesoplodon layardii*
Southern Bottlenose Whale · *Hyperoodon planifrons*
Killer Whale · *Orcinus orca*
Long-finned Pilot Whale · *Globicephala melaena*
Dusky Dolphin · *Lagenorhynchus obscurus*
Hourglass Dolphin · *Lagenorhynchus cruciger*
Peale's Porpoise · *Lagenorhynchus australis*
Commerson's Dolphin · *Cephalorynchus commersoni*
Southern Right Whale Dolphin · *Lissodelphis peronii*
Bottlenose Dolphin · *Tursiops truncatus*
Spectacled Porpoise · *Phocoena dioptrica*

Acknowledgements

For some years it has been my view that a well illustrated book, preferably with colour plates, should be produced about the Falkland Islands, for only in this format would the true image of these islands start to emerge. Attempts to sell the idea prior to 1982 were an uphill struggle and one usually met with limited interest when even the name of the Falkland Islands was mentioned.

Following the conflict of 1982 the islands were suddenly lifted out of obscurity and the project was given a new lease of life. There remained, however, my determination that such a book would have to display the islands in colour or not at all, no easy task for any publisher with any book and less so for this work, which must still be considered fairly specialist.

Help came in the form of the recently established Falkland Islands Development Corporation (FIDC) who very kindly agreed to sponsor the extra colour. To the FIDC and especially to their General Manager, Simon Armstrong, and to David St John Thomas of David & Charles who made the final decision on sponsorship arrangements, I am especially grateful.

My deep appreciation also goes to many island friends, for this work is the result of some years of travelling and seeking new images of these islands, a task which would have been far more difficult without their help.

Finally to Ann and Derek Brownson who previewed the manuscript and to Maria for her work in its preparation.

I. J. STRANGE
Falkland Islands

Index

Page numbers in *italic* indicate illustrations

159